Everyman's Poetry

Everyman, I will go with thee,
and be thy guide

Dylan Thomas

Selected and edited by WALFORD DAVIES

University of Wales, Aberystwyth

D0755458

EVERYMAN

J. M. Dent · London

This edition first published by Everyman Paperbacks in 1997
Selection, introduction and other critical apparatus
© J. M. Dent 1997

© 1937, 1945, 1955, 1956, 1962,
1965, 1967, 1971, 1977, 1997 The Trustees for
the Copyrights of Dylan Thomas

J. M. Dent
Orion Publishing Group
Orion House
5 Upper St Martin's Lane
London WC2H 9EA

Typeset by Deltatype Ltd, Birkenhead, Merseyside
Printed in Great Britain by
The Guernsey Press Co. Ltd, Guernsey, C. I.

British Library Cataloging-in-Publication Data is available
upon request.

ISBN 0 460 87831 X

Contents

Note on the Author and Editor

DYLAN MARLAIS THOMAS was born in Swansea on 27 October 1914, the son of the Senior English Master at Swansea Grammar School. After leaving that school he worked briefly as a junior reporter on the *South Wales Evening Post* before deciding to embark on a literary career in London. Here he rapidly established himself as a remarkable personality and one of the finest poets of his generation. *18 Poems* appeared in 1934, *Twenty-five Poems* in 1936, *Deaths and Entrances* in 1946 and *In Country Sleep* (in America only) in 1952. His *Collected Poems* was published in 1952. Throughout his life Thomas also wrote short stories, his most famous collection being *Portrait of the Artist as a Young Dog* (1940). He also wrote filmscripts, was a celebrated broadcaster of radio features and talks, lectured widely in America, and wrote the radio 'play for voices' *Under Milk Wood*, first broadcast posthumously in 1954. The highly successful lecturing tours of America in the early 1950s were made possible by his fame but were also necessary for financial reasons. In 1953, on the fourth of those visits, and shortly after his thirty-ninth birthday, he collapsed and died in New York. His body is buried in Wales – at Laugharne, his home for many years.

PROFESSOR WALFORD DAVIES is Director of Continuing Education at the University of Wales, Aberystwyth. His other work on Dylan Thomas includes two critical studies of the poet and the following editions: *Dylan Thomas: Early Prose Writings* (1971); *Dylan Thomas: New Critical Essays* (1972); *Deaths and Entrances* (Gregynog Press, 1984); *Dylan Thomas: Selected Poems* (1993); and, with Ralph Maud, *Dylan Thomas: Collected Poems 1934–1953* (1988) and *Under Milk Wood* (1995).

Chronology of Dylan Thomas's Life

Year	Life
27 Oct 1914	Dylan Marlais Thomas born in Swansea
Sept 1925	Enters Swansea Grammar School, where his father was Senior English Master
27 Apr 1930	Starts the first of the 'Notebooks' into which he copied his early poems. (The Notebooks continued until Apr 1934)
Aug 1931	Leaves school. Employed as Reporter on the *South Wales Evening Post* (until Dec 1932)
Mar 1933	First poem published in London ('And death shall have no dominion' in the *New English Weekly*)
Aug 1933	First visit to London
Sept 1933	First poems published in 'Poet's Corner' of the *Sunday Referee* ('That Sanity be Kept'). Correspondence with Pamela Hansford Johnson begins
22 Apr 1934	Wins Book Prize of the 'Poet's Corner' – i.e., the *Sunday Referee's* sponsorship of his first collection of poems
Feb–Nov 1934	Several visits to London
10 Nov 1934	Moves to live in London
18 Dec 1934	*18 Poems* published
Apr 1936	Meets Caitlin Macnamara
10 Sept 1936	*Twenty-five Poems* published
21 Apr 1937	First radio broadcast ('Life and the Modern Poet')
11 Jul 1937	Marries Caitlin Macnamara
May 1938	First moved to live in Laugharne, Carmarthenshire
30 Jan 1939	First son (Llewelyn) born, in Hampshire
24 Aug 1939	*The Map of Love* (poems and stories) published
20 Dec 1939	*The World I Breathe* (a selection of his poetry and prose) – his first volume publication in America

Year	Life
4 Apr 1940	*Portrait of the Artist as a Young Dog* (short stories) published
July 1940	Leaves Laugharne for London
Sept 1940	Begins work as script-writer for films with the Strand Film Company
1940–2	Living partly in London, partly in Wales
Late 1942	Brings wife and son to live in Chelsea
Feb 1943	*New Poems* (USA)
3 Mar 1943	Daughter (Aeronwy) born
1943	Continuous work as broadcaster begins
Sept 1944 –summer 1945	Living at New Quay, Cardiganshire
Summer 1945 –spring 1946	Living in London
7 Feb 1946	*Deaths and Entrances* published
Mar 1946 –May 1949	Living in or near Oxford
8 Nov 1946	*Selected Writings* (USA)
Apr–Aug 1947	Visits Italy
Sept 1947	Moves to live in South Leigh, Oxfordshire
1948	Writing feature films for Gainsborough
Mar 1949	Visits Prague as guest of Czechoslovak government
May 1949	Laugharne again becomes his main home (The Boat House)
24 Jul 1949	Second son (Colm) born
Feb–Jun 1950	First American tour
Jan 1951	In Iran, writing film script for the Anglo Iranian Oil Company
Jan–May 1952	Second American tour
Feb 1952	*In Country Sleep* (USA)
10 Nov 1952	*Collected Poems 1934–1952* published
16 Dec 1952	The poet's father dies
31 Mar 1953	*Collected Poems* (USA)
Apr–Jun 1953	Third American tour
14 May 1953	First performance of *Under Milk Wood* in New York
14 May 1953	*The Doctor and the Devils.* The first of the film scripts to be published
Oct 1953	Leaves on final American tour
9 Nov 1953	Dies in St Vincent's Hospital, New York City

Introduction

When the poetry of the nineteen-year-old Dylan Thomas burst onto the London literary scene in 1933, one of the first to recognize the portent was the major English critic, William Empson. The impact was soon consolidated with the publication of Thomas's first volume, *18 Poems*, in December 1934. Twenty years later in 1954, with Thomas dead the previous year at the age of thirty-nine, Empson reviewed the *Collected Poems*:

> It is the first inspiration, the poems the young man hit the town with (overwhelmingly good, though one resisted them because one couldn't see why), which are the permanent challenge to a critic and in a way the decisive part of his work. I was disinclined to review the *Collected Poems* when it came out during his lifetime, because I would have had to say I liked the early obscure ones best, and I was afraid this would distress him; so I now have one of those unavailing regrets about my timidity, because he knew all that kind of thing very well and could be distressed only by a refusal to say it . . . What hit the town of London was the child Dylan publishing 'The force that through the green fuse' as a prize poem in the *Sunday Referee* [October 1933], and from that day he was a famous poet; I think the incident does some credit to the town, making it look less clumsy than you would think.

Empson obviously had the highest respect not only for Thomas's genius but for his artistic integrity and personal likeability, aspects too often obscured by the legend of the bohemian drunkard that ultimately took over. But Empson makes three other points of particular interest. He emphasizes Thomas's youth ('the child Dylan'), his outsiderness (he was someone who 'hit the town'), and the relationship between the earlier and the later work. All three points are relevant to any selection seeking to represent Dylan Thomas's achievement as a poet.

The earliness of the impact was the result of the young man's unusually strong ambition in the first place to be a poet. His father, a senior Grammar School English teacher in Swansea, had also had

poetic ambitions. He delighted in reciting English verse, especially
Shakespeare, to the young Dylan long before the boy was reading
poetry for himself. So a strong aural appeal was there from the start.
But the boy's own powers also took early form, in poems entered
regularly into four school exercise books between 1930 and 1934,
covering the age of sixteen to twenty, bridging Thomas's last year
at Swansea Grammar School, his first brief job as a reporter on the
local newspaper, and his first visits to London. These now famous
'Notebooks' were like an inner circle within circles. Here were
remarkable, privately driven poems by a teenager, often pretending
to be ill at home in order to write them, pampered by his mother in a
small but comfortable suburban home, in a provincial town – and a
provincial town in Wales. Thomas himself would not have called it
'comfortable'; hence his sharp poem at the age of nineteen, 'I have
longed to move away' –

> I have longed to move away
> From the repetition of salutes,
> For there are ghosts in the air
> And ghostly echoes on paper,
> And the thunder of calls and notes.

But the very isolation afforded by puritan-suburban Swansea from
the fashionable call of London ('the thunder of calls and notes') was
the very thing that enabled him to develop a personal voice of
highly original timbre on very private subjects. Most of his English
poetic contemporaries – the Auden group at Oxford, for example –
had already been many years at boarding school and university,
their very education geared to essentially 'public' concerns, and
with easy access to cosmopolitan London. In the early years of
those blatantly politicized thirties, poems like 'And death shall have
no dominion', 'My hero bares his nerves' and 'The force that
through the green fuse' must have seemed to blow in from
nowhere. They hit a London absorbed in its own fashions and
sealed against its own regions. V. S. Pritchet had already mused in
his influential column in the *New Statesman* that 'if anything has
died in the last thirty years, it is regionalism. Our society – why
pretend – has made a war on regionalism and has destroyed it'.

Whether this was politically true, or even culturally possible, is
doubtful. But in 1933 poems by an unknown Welshman needed a
particularly strong profile to be even visible from London. And at

that time London was the only place in which to be published. The strength of the impact of *18 Poems* is shown in the fact that Thomas, at only twenty years of age, was considered ahead of no-one less than W. B. Yeats as a possible editor for *The Oxford Book of Modern Verse*. The provincial pup who later titled his auto-biography a *Portrait of the Artist as a Young Dog* (1940) was already ready, as he quipped, to 'astound the salons and the cliques/Of half-wits, publicists and freaks'. But his impact on London was not any shallow opportunism, just as an *Oxford Book of Modern Verse* by Thomas would have been much less contentious than the one Yeats finally published in 1936. Thomas's own poetry had quickly developed an original voice. Its origins may have seemed difficult to explain but its meticulous forms and rhetoric were clearly tradi-tional. The late romanticism of the first two notebooks had given way to imitations of the thin-lipped Imagists, of the urban seediness of early Eliot, and of the rhythmic breathlessness of Hopkins. All good apprentice stuff. But, even in forsaking those influences, the notebooks never abandoned a crucial principle of all poetry, Modernist or traditional: that its power lies in images, not abstractions.

But then, quite suddenly, there was also this:

> Before I knocked and flesh let enter,
> With liquid hands tapped on the womb,
> I who was shapeless as the water
> That shaped the Jordan near my home
> Was brother to Mnetha's daughter
> And sister to the fathering worm.

What changed most decisively in the last two notebooks was the very world in which the poetry moved. We all know where we biologically come from, but have we ever tried to imagine our way back into the mystery? Suddenly, here was a teenager celebrating the creation of the world, the relationship between world and word, and the sheer magic of prenatal existence in the womb – all the miracles we duly, and dully, take for granted.

On discovering this kind of material, Thomas's cultural 'outsider-ness' also came into play. The simple fact is that the young man was Welsh. Both his parents were in fact Welsh-speaking. They were first-generation working-class products of Welsh rural Carmarthen-shire and of the drift eastward to the slowly Anglicizing towns of industrial Glamorganshire. The very names of those old counties now sound like something out of distant history, a feeling that was even then part of the young poet's legacy:

> Hold hard, these ancient minutes in the cuckoo's month,
> Under the lank, fourth folly on Glamorgan's hill . . .

Ever since the end of the previous century, the move eastwards had been the result of the need to secure jobs. But as a first-class Honours graduate in English of the University College of Wales at Aberystwyth the poet's father saw it also as a means of 'getting on' in the world. When he ended up as a respected Grammar School master in Swansea, he decided that Dylan and his sister should not be saddled with the Welsh language, and that their English should even have the further advantage of elocution lessons. This is what produced what Thomas called his 'cut-glass' accent, so memorably recorded in the rich but slightly clipped voice of his poetry-readings and broadcasts. But it was Welsh that the parents spoke to each other, and Thomas's father even went out in the evenings to teach Welsh in adult education classes. In such a lineage, the young Dylan was caught between two cultures, in a creative fracture between the English of the poems and the Welshness that gives them their edge and excitement.

The result, at its simplest, is an 'external' ability to see possibilities of idiom and phrasing that would not even occur to a more thoroughly 'English' poet, who would be likely to take the language very much more for granted. In Thomas's language, ordinary phrases like *wild strawberries* and *innocent boys* become 'wild boys innocent as strawberries'; *the west wind* and *the man in the moon* become 'the man in the wind and the west moon'. Or consider the poem Empson remembers taking London by storm, 'The force that through the green fuse' –

> The force that drives the water through the rocks
> Drives my red blood; that dries the mouthing streams
> Turns mine to wax.

The poet sees, quite objectively, that the coagulation of blood can be matched in the sequence 'drives . . . drives . . . dries'. But he also sees that 'wax' is a word that can signify *growth* (as in 'to wax bold') as well as *arrest* (as in the tallow of a candle). And this sense of both *driving* and *drying* is crucial in a poem concerned with the endless cycle of creation and decreation. The same pun is made in another poem of the same period, 'Light breaks where no sun shines': 'Where no wax is, the candle shows its hairs.' English was the only language the Welshman knew. But, like the Irish Joyce, he seems to be taking creative revenge on it.

Yet paradoxically – at one remove – he was also influenced by the Welsh-language poetic tradition in its respect for difficult, ornately crafted verse-forms. Good examples are the rhyme-scheme of 'Prologue', the internal rhyme-scheme of 'The conversation of prayers', or the intricate patterns of assonance with which 'Poem in October' and 'Fern Hill' are structured. Or consider how the first stanza of 'Before I knocked', quoted above (p. xi), sets in motion the first three of no fewer than twenty-three lines ending in 'er', and yet still has enough energy left to plant 'er' words even *inside* that stanza:

> Was broth*er* to Mnetha's daught*er*
> And sist*er* to the fathering worm.

It is in this way that Thomas's Welshness manifests itself. He abandoned what he called the 'mainly free verse' poems of the earlier notebooks. Free verse belonged to other cultures; it is not congenial to the Welsh poetic temperament. And added to the Welshness of intricate verse forms were also the strong rhythms of the Bible, with the repetitive units that again bring pressure to bear on single words. What we have here, at base, is an endless appetite for the essential musicality of language – what Thomas once called 'the colour of saying' – the auditory power that language can have in and for itself. In another magical phrase, he called it the need for poetry to be 'heavy in tare, though nimble'. This weight and density of texture and musical movement were exactly what was reacted against after his death by the more 'intellectual' English poets of the 1950s, such as Philip Larkin, Donald Davie and John Wain, enamoured of more modest verse-forms, of understatement and irony. These in fact were often poets who, a decade earlier, when they themselves were starting to write in the early 1940s, had admired Thomas above all others. He was, after all, only marginally older. Thomas's early death made him doubly potent: his exciting poetic skills were, within a decade, both emulated and reacted against.

But a similar reaction had long since occurred within Thomas himself. The 1938 poem 'Once it was the colour of saying' shows the twenty-four-year-old determined to tone down the independent suggestiveness of words into something more austere, and to change from medium to message:

> Once it was the colour of saying
> Soaked my table the uglier shade of a hill . . .
>
> Now my saying shall be my undoing
> And every stone I wind off like a reel.

Twenty-four may seem a young age for a major shift in career. But by that age Thomas had already written well over a half of all the poems he was ever going to. He was of course to die at the age of thirty-nine, but that is not the only thing that explains the front-loading of the career. The sheer productiveness of the early notebooks gave him an embarrassingly rich store from which to draw for his first three volumes: *18 Poems* (1934), *Twenty-five Poems* (1936) and *The Map of Love* (1939). And despite the urge towards greater austerity and objectivity, his delight in the music of verse and in complex verse forms increased rather than lessened. The result was fewer poems. Yeats once wrote that 'A line will take us hours maybe'; increasingly for Thomas a line, or a single word or sound within a line, took months.

And yet, around the age of twenty-four, something did change. The themes of creation and process began to merge into more objective subjects such as the poet's response to individuals, events and landscapes in the external everyday world. The change in simple subject-matter was strengthened by a parallel change in the prose works. Between 1938 and 1940 the arcane subjects and surrealism of the early short stories were replaced by the wonderful comic realism of the autobiographical short stories of *Portrait of the Artist as a Young Dog* (1940), describing the sharp adventures of the Swansea ragamuffin and poet-to-be. But the poetry was not only taken over, it was also overtaken, by events. Beyond 1938, the poet's marriage and parenthood, and the gathering storm of war, made it natural for him to be drawn to more immediately shareable subjects. Hence such poems as those to his wife and children or his maternal aunt, Ann Jones. The latter poem, 'After the funeral', Thomas described as 'the only one I have written that is, directly, about the life and death of one particular human being I knew – and not about the very many lives and deaths whether seen, as in my first poems, in the tumultous world of my own being or, as in the later poems, in war, grief, and the great holes and corners of universal love':

> I know her scrubbed and sour humble hands
> Lie with religion in their cramp, her threadbare
> Whisper in a damp word, her wits drilled hollow,
> Her fist of a face died clenched on a round pain
> And sculptured Ann is seventy years of stone.

But the deaths of unknown people lost in the Second World War – in poems such as 'There was a saviour', 'Ceremony After a Fire Raid' and 'A Refusal to Mourn the Death, by Fire, of a Child in London' – took him just as decisively out of himself. Indeed, the experience of the bombing raids that devastated so much of London and his home town of Swansea, coupled with the news slowly emerging of the concentration camps and the arrival in 1945 of a period terrorized to the end of his lifetime and beyond by the threat of the nuclear destruction of the whole world, gave the late poetry one pervasive theme. That theme was the search for a lost innocence. This was the point where the prose had in turn suddenly to catch up with the poetry. For example, the famous 'play for voices', *Under Milk Wood*, with its celebration of 'a place of love', is an extension of the main concern of the later poems. It is a concern that explains the essentially rural, pastoral idiom of all the later poetry, starting with the brilliantly shareable evocations of a lost childhood in poems such as 'Fern Hill' and 'Poem in October'. The philosopher Theodor Adorno said that lyric poetry was impossible after Auschwitz. But Thomas's poetry after 1945 was already a reaction to the obscenity of holocaust. It sought to recreate, and hang on to, the very norms by which we recognize that obscenity. Thomas himself said that holocaust was central to the poetry. He explained the heart of 'Poem on his Birthday' as follows:

> he, who is progressing, afraid, to his own fiery end in the cloud of an atomic explosion knows that, out at sea, animals who attack and eat other sea animals are tasting the flesh of their own death . . . His death lurks for him, and for all, in the next lunatic war.

So, to raise the whole question, as William Empson does, of whether we prefer the earlier or the later poems is to focus the huge distance this brief career travelled, from adolescent self-consciousness to magnanimous love. Empson's own preference for 'the early obscure ones' is understandable in that they still set up the most immediate challenge ('overwhelmingly good, though one resisted them because one couldn't see why'). But an equally cogent vote would now go for the larger, more shareable later poems where a sense of elegiac acceptance is projected onto recognizable landscapes and seascapes. But in a way, early or late, it is the same world-view: a vision of the place of human consciousness within a physical world from which human consciousness cannot ever really divorce itself:

> And I am dumb to tell the crooked rose
> My youth is bent by the same wintry fever.

And again, early or late, what underpins it all is Thomas's commitment to the hard *craft* of poetry – the commitment so memorably affirmed in 'In my craft or sullen art'.

To quote such a major poet-critic as Empson is to quote the keenest possible witness from within the very period in which the career of Dylan Thomas took off, took shape, and ended. Empson's view helps us place that career in the historic context that is now part of its meaning. And perhaps most relevant of all in this respect is Empson's first-hand confirmation of a particular aspect of Dylan Thomas's character *as a man*:

I am trying to consider a reader who is doubtful whether to read this poetry, so I am thinking whether I could give any useful advice. You must realise that he was a very witty man, with a very keen though not at all poisoned recognition that the world contains horror as well as delight; his chief power as a stylist is to convey a sickened loathing which somehow at once (within the phrase) enforces a welcome for the eternal necessities of the world.

WALFORD DAVIES

Dylan Thomas

Prologue

This day winding down now
At God speeded summer's end
In the torrent salmon sun,
In my seashaken house
On a breakneck of rocks
Tangled with chirrup and fruit,
Froth, flute, fin and quill
At a wood's dancing hoof,
By scummed, starfish sands
With their fishwife cross   10
Gulls, pipers, cockles, and sails,
Out there, crow black, men
Tackled with clouds, who kneel
To the sunset nets,
Geese nearly in heaven, boys
Stabbing, and herons, and shells
That speak seven seas,
Eternal waters away
From the cities of nine
Days' night whose towers will catch   20
In the religious wind
Like stalks of tall, dry straw,
At poor peace I sing
To you, strangers, (though song
Is a burning and crested act,
The fire of birds in
The world's turning wood,
For my sawn, splay sounds),
Out of these seathumbed leaves
That will fly and fall   30
Like leaves of trees and as soon
Crumble and undie
Into the dogdayed night.
Seaward the salmon, sucked sun slips,
And the dumb swans drub blue

My dabbed bay's dusk, as I hack
This rumpus of shapes
For you to know
How I, a spinning man,
Glory also this star, bird   40
Roared, sea born, man torn, blood blest.
Hark: I trumpet the place,
From fish to jumping hill! Look:
I build my bellowing ark
To the best of my love
As the flood begins,
Out of the fountainhead
Of fear, rage red, manalive,
Molten and mountainous to stream
Over the wound asleep   50
Sheep white hollow farms

To Wales in my arms.
Hoo, there, in castle keep,
You king singsong owls, who moonbeam
The flickering runs and dive
The dingle furred deer dead!
Huloo, on plumbed bryns,
O my ruffled ring dove
In the hooting, nearly dark
With Welsh and reverent rook,   60
Coo rooing the woods' praise,
Who moons her blue notes from her nest
Down to the curlew herd!
Ho, hullaballoing clan
Agape, with woe
In your beaks, on the gabbing capes!
Heigh, on horseback hill, jack
Whisking hare! who
Hears, there, this fox light, my flood ship's
Clangour as I hew and smite   70
(A clash of anvils for my
Hubbub and fiddle, this tune
On a tongued puffball)
But animals thick as thieves

On God's rough tumbling grounds
(Hail to His beasthood!).
Beasts who sleep good and thin,
Hist, in hogsback woods! The haystacked
Hollow farms in a throng
Of waters cluck and cling,   80
And barnroofs cockcrow war!
O kingdom of neighbours, finned
Felled and quilled, flash to my patch
Work ark and the moonshine
Drinking Noah of the bay,
With pelt, and scale, and fleece:
Only the drowned deep bells
Of sheep and churches noise
Poor peace as the sun sets
And dark shoals every holy field.   90
We shall ride out alone, and then,
Under the stars of Wales,
Cry, Multitudes of arks! Across
The water lidded lands,
Manned with their loves they'll move,
Like wooden islands, hill to hill.
Huloo, my prowed dove with a flute!
Ahoy, old, sea-legged fox,
Tom tit and Dai mouse!
My ark sings in the sun   100
At God speeded summer's end
And the flood flowers now.

The spire cranes

The spire cranes. Its statue is an aviary.
From the stone nest it does not let the feathery
Carved birds blunt their striking throats on the salt gravel,
Pierce the spilt sky with diving wing in weed and heel
An inch in froth. Chimes cheat the prison spire, pelter
In time like outlaw rains on that priest, water,
Time for the swimmers' hands, music for silver lock
And mouth. Both note and plume plunge from the spire's
    hook.
Those craning birds are choice for you, songs that jump back
To the built voice, or fly with winter to the bells,
But do not travel down dumb wind like prodigals.

Out of the sighs

Out of the sighs a little comes,
But not of grief, for I have knocked down that
Before the agony; the spirit grows,
Forgets, and cries;
A little comes, is tasted and found good;
All could not disappoint;
There must, be praised, some certainty,
If not of loving well, then not,
And that is true after perpetual defeat.

After such fighting as the weakest know,　　　　10
There's more than dying;
Lose the great pains or stuff the wound,
He'll ache too long
Through no regret of leaving woman waiting
For her soldier stained with spilt words
That spill such acrid blood.

Were that enough, enough to ease the pain,
Feeling regret when this is wasted
That made me happy in the sun,
And, sleeping, made me dream　　　　20
How much was happy while it lasted,
Were vaguenesses enough and the sweet lies plenty,
The hollow words could bear all suffering
And cure me of ills.

Were that enough, bone, blood, and sinew,
The twisted brain, the fair-formed loin,
Groping for matter under the dog's plate,
Man should be cured of distemper.
For all there is to give I offer:
Crumbs, barn, and halter.　　　　30

I have longed to move away

I have longed to move away
From the hissing of the spent lie
And the old terrors' continual cry
Growing more terrible as the day
Goes over the hill into the deep sea;
I have longed to move away
From the repetition of salutes,
For there are ghosts in the air
And ghostly echoes on paper,
And the thunder of calls and notes.   10

I have longed to move away but am afraid;
Some life, yet unspent, might explode
Out of the old lie burning on the ground,
And, crackling into the air, leave me half-blind.
Neither by night's ancient fear,
The parting of hat from hair,
Pursed lips at the receiver,
Shall I fall to death's feather.
By these I would not care to die,
Half convention and half lie.   20

And death shall have no dominion

And death shall have no dominion.
Dead men naked they shall be one
With the man in the wind and the west moon;
When their bones are picked clean and the clean bones gone,
They shall have stars at elbow and foot;
Though they go mad they shall be sane,
Though they sink through the sea they shall rise again;
Though lovers be lost love shall not;
And death shall have no dominion.

And death shall have no dominion.   10
Under the windings of the sea
They lying long shall not die windily;
Twisting on racks when sinews give way,
Strapped to a wheel, yet they shall not break;
Faith in their hands shall snap in two,
And the unicorn evils run them through;
Split all ends up they shan't crack;
And death shall have no dominion.

And death shall have no dominion.
No more may gulls cry at their ears   20
Or waves break loud on the seashores;
Where blew a flower may a flower no more
Lift its head to the blows of the rain;
Though they be mad and dead as nails,
Heads of the characters hammer through daisies;
Break in the sun till the sun breaks down,
And death shall have no dominion.

We lying by seasand

We lying by seasand, watching yellow
And the grave sea, mock who deride
Who follow the red rivers, hollow
Alcove of words out of cicada shade,
For in this yellow grave of sand and sea
A calling for colour calls with the wind
That's grave and gay as grave and sea
Sleeping on either hand.
The lunar silences, the silent tide
Lapping the still canals, the dry tide-master   10
Ribbed between desert and water storm,
Should cure our ills of the water
With a one-coloured calm;
The heavenly music over the sand
Sounds with the grains as they hurry
Hiding the golden mountains and mansions
Of the grave, gay, seaside land.
Bound by a sovereign strip, we lie,
Watch yellow, wish for wind to blow away
The strata of the shore and drown red rock;   20
But wishes breed not, neither
Can we fend off rock arrival,
Lie watching yellow until the golden weather
Breaks, O my heart's blood, like a heart and hill.

Here in this spring

Here in this spring, stars float along the void;
Here in this ornamental winter
Down pelts the naked weather;
This summer buries a spring bird.

Symbols are selected from the years'
Slow rounding of four seasons' coasts,
In autumn teach three seasons' fires
And four birds' notes.

I should tell summer from the trees, the worms
Tell, if at all, the winter's storms   10
Or the funeral of the sun;
I should learn spring by the cuckooing,
And the slug should teach me destruction.

A worm tells summer better than the clock,
The slug's a living calendar of days;
What shall it tell me if a timeless insect
Says the world wears away?

Ears in the turrets hear

Ears in the turrets hear
Hands grumble on the door,
Eyes in the gables see
The fingers at the locks.
Shall I unbolt or stay
Alone till the day I die
Unseen by stranger-eyes
In this white house?
Hands, hold you poison or grapes?

Beyond this island bound   10
By a thin sea of flesh
And a bone coast,
The land lies out of sound
And the hills out of mind.
No bird or flying fish
Disturbs this island's rest.

Ears in this island hear
The wind pass like a fire,
Eyes in this island see
Ships anchor off the bay.   20
Shall I run to the ships
With the wind in my hair,
Or stay till the day I die
And welcome no sailor?
Ships, hold you poison or grapes?

Hands grumble on the door,
Ships anchor off the bay,
Rain beats the sand and slates.
Shall I let in the stranger,
Shall I welcome the sailor,   30
Or stay till the day I die?

Hands of the stranger and holds of the ships,
Hold you poison or grapes?

Why east wind chills

Why east wind chills and south wind cools
Shall not be known till windwell dries
And west's no longer drowned
In winds that bring the fruit and rind
Of many a hundred falls;
Why silk is soft and the stone wounds
The child shall question all his days,
Why night-time rain and the breast's blood
Both quench his thirst he'll have a black reply.

When cometh Jack Frost? the children ask.   10
Shall they clasp a comet in their fists?
Not till, from high and low, their dust
Sprinkles in children's eyes a long-last sleep
And dusk is crowded with the children's ghosts,
Shall a white answer echo from the rooftops.

All things are known: the stars' advice
Calls some content to travel with the winds,
Though what the stars ask as they round
Time upon time the towers of the skies
Is heard but little till the stars go out.   20

I hear content, and 'Be content'
Ring like a handbell through the corridors,
And 'Know no answer,' and I know
No answer to the children's cry
Of echo's answer and the man of frost
And ghostly comets over the raised fists.

The hand that signed the paper

The hand that signed the paper felled a city;
Five sovereign fingers taxed the breath,
Doubled the globe of dead and halved a country;
These five kings did a king to death.

The mighty hand leads to a sloping shoulder,
The finger joints are cramped with chalk;
A goose's quill has put an end to murder
That put an end to talk.

The hand that signed the treaty bred a fever,
And famine grew, and locusts came;   10
Great is the hand that holds dominion over
Man by a scribbled name.

The five kings count the dead but do not soften
The crusted wound nor stroke the brow;
A hand rules pity as a hand rules heaven;
Hands have no tears to flow.

Before I knocked

Before I knocked and flesh let enter,
With liquid hands tapped on the womb,
I who was shapeless as the water
That shaped the Jordan near my home
Was brother to Mnetha's daughter
And sister to the fathering worm.

I who was deaf to spring and summer,
Who knew not sun nor moon by name,
Felt thud beneath my flesh's armour,
As yet was in a moltern form,   10
The leaden stars, the rainy hammer
Swung by my father from his dome.

I knew the message of the winter,
The darted hail, the childish snow,
And the wind was my sister suitor;
Wind in me leaped, the hellborn dew;
My veins flowed with the Eastern weather;
Ungotten I knew night and day.

As yet ungotten, I did suffer;
The rack of dreams my lily bones   20
Did twist into a living cipher,
And flesh was snipped to cross the lines
Of gallow crosses on the liver
And brambles in the wringing brains.

My throat knew thirst before the structure
Of skin and vein around the well
Where words and water make a mixture
Unfailing till the blood runs foul;
My heart knew love, my belly hunger;
I smelt the maggot in my stool.   30

And time cast forth my mortal creature
To drift or drown upon the seas
Acquainted with the salt adventure
Of tides that never touch the shores.
I who was rich was made the richer
By sipping at the vine of days.

I, born of flesh and ghost, was neither
A ghost nor man, but mortal ghost.
And I was struck down by death's feather.
I was mortal to the last   40
Long breath that carried to my father
The message of his dying christ.

You who bow down at cross and altar,
Remember me and pity Him
Who took my flesh and bone for armour
And doublecrossed my mother's womb.

My hero bares his nerves

My hero bares his nerves along my wrist
That rules from wrist to shoulder,
Unpacks the head that, like a sleepy ghost,
Leans on my mortal ruler,
The proud spine spurning turn and twist.

And these poor nerves so wired to the skull
Ache on the lovelorn paper
I hug to love with my unruly scrawl
That utters all love hunger
And tells the page the empty ill.   10

My hero bares my side and sees his heart
Tread, like a naked Venus,
The beach of flesh, and wind her bloodred plait;
Stripping my loin of promise,
He promises a secret heat.

He holds the wire from this box of nerves
Praising the mortal error
Of birth and death, the two sad knaves of thieves,
And the hunger's emperor;
He pulls the chain, the cistern moves.   20

The force that through the green fuse

The force that through the green fuse drives the flower
Drives my green age; that blasts the roots of trees
Is my destroyer.
And I am dumb to tell the crooked rose
My youth is bent by the same wintry fever.

The force that drives the water through the rocks
Drives my red blood; that dries the mouthing streams
Turns mine to wax.
And I am dumb to mouth unto my veins
How at the mountain spring the same mouth sucks.   10

The hand that whirls the water in the pool
Stirs the quicksand; that ropes the blowing wind
Hauls my shroud sail.
And I am dumb to tell the hanging man
How of my clay is made the hangman's lime.

The lips of time leech to the fountain head;
Love drips and gathers, but the fallen blood
Shall calm her sores.
And I am dumb to tell a weather's wind
How time has ticked a heaven round the stars.   20

And I am dumb to tell the lover's tomb
How at my sheet goes the same crooked worm.

That sanity be kept

That sanity be kept I sit at open windows,
Regard the sky, make unobtrusive comment on the moon,
Sit at open windows in my shirt,
And let the traffic pass, the signals shine,
The engines run, the brass bands keep in tune,
For sanity must be preserved.

Thinking of death, I sit and watch the park
Where children play in all their innocence,
And matrons on the littered grass
Absorb the daily sun.   10

The sweet suburban music from a hundred lawns
Comes softly to my ears. The English mowers mow and mow.

I mark the couples walking arm in arm,
Observe their smiles,
Sweet invitations and inventions,
See them lend love illustration
By gesture and grimace.
I watch them curiously, detect beneath the laughs
What stands for grief, a vague bewilderment
At things not turning right.   20

I sit at open windows in my shirt,
Observe, like some Jehovah of the west
What passes by, that sanity be kept.

In the beginning

In the beginning was the three-pointed star,
One smile of light across the empty face;
One bough of bone across the rooting air,
The substance forked that marrowed the first sun;
And, burning ciphers on the round of space,
Heaven and hell mixed as they spun.

In the beginning was the pale signature,
Three-syllabled and starry as the smile;
And after came the imprints on the water,
Stamp of the minted face upon the moon;   10
The blood that touched the crosstree and the grail
Touched the first cloud and left a sign.

In the beginning was the mounting fire
That set alight the weathers from a spark,
A three-eyed, red-eyed spark, blunt as a flower;
Life rose and sprouted from the rolling seas,
Burst in the roots, pumped from the earth and rock
The secret oils that drive the grass.

In the beginning was the word, the word
That from the solid bases of the light   20
Abstracted all the letters of the void;
And from the cloudy bases of the breath
The word flowed up, translating to the heart
First characters of birth and death.

In the beginning was the secret brain.
The brain was celled and soldered in the thought
Before the pitch was forking to a sun;
Before the veins were shaking in their sieve,
Blood shot and scattered to the winds of light
The ribbed original of love.   30

Light breaks where no sun shines

Light breaks where no sun shines;
Where no sea runs, the waters of the heart
Push in their tides;
And, broken ghosts with glow-worms in their heads,
The things of light
File through the flesh where no flesh decks the bones.

A candle in the thighs
Warms youth and seed and burns the seeds of age;
Where no seed stirs,
The fruit of man unwrinkles in the stars,   10
Bright as a fig;
Where no wax is, the candle shows its hairs.

Dawn breaks behind the eyes;
From poles of skull and toe the windy blood
Slides like a sea;
Nor fenced, nor staked, the gushers of the sky
Spout to the rod
Divining in a smile the oil of tears.

Night in the sockets rounds,
Like some pitch moon, the limit of the globes;   20
Day lights the bone;
Where no cold is, the skinning gales unpin
The winter's robes;
The film of spring is hanging from the lids.

Light breaks on secret lots,
On tips of thought where thoughts smell in the rain;
When logics die,
The secret of the soil grows through the eye,
And blood jumps in the sun;
Above the waste allotments the dawn halts.   30

This bread I break

This bread I break was once the oat,
The wine upon a foreign tree
Plunged in its fruit;
Man in the day or wind at night
Laid the crops low, broke the grape's joy.

Once in this wine the summer blood
Knocked in the flesh that decked the vine,
Once in this bread
The oat was merry in the wind;
Man broke the sun, pulled the wind down.   10

This flesh you break, this blood you let
Make desolation in the vein,
Were oat and grape
Born of the sensual root and sap;
My wine you drink, my bread you snap.

When once the twilight locks

When once the twilight locks no longer
Locked in the long worm of my finger
Nor dammed the sea that sped about my fist,
The mouth of time sucked, like a sponge,
The milky acid on each hinge,
And swallowed dry the waters of the breast.

When the galactic sea was sucked
And all the dry seabed unlocked,
I sent my creature scouting on the globe,
That globe itself of hair and bone   10
That, sewn to me by nerve and brain,
Had stringed my flask of matter to his rib.

My fuses timed to charge his heart,
He blew like powder to the light
And held a little sabbath with the sun,
But when the stars, assuming shape,
Drew in his eyes the straws of sleep,
He drowned his father's magics in a dream.

All issue armoured, of the grave,
The redhaired cancer still alive,   20
The cataracted eyes that filmed their cloth;
Some dead undid their bushy jaws,
And bags of blood let out their flies;
He had by heart the Christ-cross-row of death.

Sleep navigates the tides of time;
The dry Sargasso of the tomb
Gives up its dead to such a working sea;
And sleep rolls mute above the beds
Where fishes' food is fed the shades
Who periscope through flowers to the sky.   30

The hanged who lever from the limes
Ghostly propellers for their limbs,
The cypress lads who wither with the cock,
These, and the others in sleep's acres,
Of dreaming men make moony suckers,
And snipe the fools of vision in the back.

When once the twilight screws were turned,
And mother milk was stiff as sand,
I sent my own ambassador to light;
By trick or chance he fell asleep   40
And conjured up a carcase shape
To rob me of my fluids in his heart.

Awake, my sleeper, to the sun,
A worker in the morning town,
And leave the poppied pickthank where he lies;
The fences of the light are down,
All but the briskest riders thrown,
And worlds hang on the trees.

Where once the waters of your face

Where once the waters of your face
Spun to my screws, your dry ghost blows,
The dead turns up its eye;
Where once the mermen through your ice
Pushed up their hair, the dry wind steers
Through salt and root and roe.

Where once your green knots sank their splice
Into the tided cord, there goes
The green unraveller,
His scissors oiled, his knife hung loose   10
To cut the channels at their source
And lay the wet fruits low.

Invisible, your clocking tides
Break on the lovebeds of the weeds;
The weed of love's left dry;
There round about your stones the shades
Of children go who, from their voids,
Cry to the dolphined sea.

Dry as a tomb, your coloured lids
Shall not be latched while magic glides   20
Sage on the earth and sky;
There shall be corals in your beds,
There shall be serpents in your tides,
Till all our sea-faiths die.

Our eunuch dreams

I

Our eunuch dreams, all seedless in the light,
Of light and love, the tempers of the heart,
Whack their boys' limbs,
And, winding-footed in their shawl and sheet,
Groom the dark brides, the widows of the night
Fold in their arms.

The shades of girls, all flavoured from their shrouds,
When sunlight goes are sundered from the worm,
The bones of men, the broken in their beds,
By midnight pulleys that unhouse the tomb.   10

II

In this our age the gunman and his moll,
Two one-dimensioned ghosts, love on a reel,
Strange to our solid eye,
And speak their midnight nothings as they swell;
When cameras shut they hurry to their hole
Down in the yard of day.

They dance between their arclamps and our skull,
Impose their shots, throwing the nights away;
We watch the show of shadows kiss or kill,
Flavoured of celluloid give love the lie.   20

III

Which is the world? Of our two sleepings, which
Shall fall awake when cures and their itch
Raise up this red-eyed earth?
Pack off the shapes of daylight and their starch,
The sunny gentlemen, the Welshing rich,
Or drive the night-geared forth.

The photograph is married to the eye,
Grafts on its bride one-sided skins of truth;

The dream has sucked the sleeper of his faith
That shrouded men might marrow as they fly.   30

IV

This is the world: the lying likeness of
Our strips of stuff that tatter as we move
Loving and being loth;
The dream that kicks the buried from their sack
And lets their trash be honoured as the quick.
This is the world. Have faith.

For we shall be a shouter like the cock,
Blowing the old dead back; our shots shall smack
The image from the plates;
And we shall be fit fellows for a life,   40
And who remain shall flower as they love,
Praise to our faring hearts.

I see the boys of summer

I

I see the boys of summer in their ruin
Lay the gold tithings barren,
Setting no store by harvest, freeze the soils;
There in their heat the winter floods
Of frozen loves they fetch their girls,
And drown the cargoed apples in their tides.

These boys of light are curdlers in their folly,
Sour the boiling honey;
The jacks of frost they finger in the hives;
There in the sun the frigid threads   10
Of doubt and dark they feed their nerves;
The signal moon is zero in their voids.

I see the summer children in their mothers
Split up the brawned womb's weathers,
Divide the night and day with fairy thumbs;
There in the deep with quartered shades
Of sun and moon they paint their dams
As sunlight paints the shelling of their heads.

I see that from these boys shall men of nothing
Stature by seedy shifting.   20
Or lame the air with leaping from its heats;
There from their hearts the dogdayed pulse
Of love and light bursts in their throats.
O see the pulse of summer in the ice.

II

But seasons must be challenged or they totter
Into a chiming quarter
Where, punctual as death, we ring the stars;
There, in his night, the black-tongued bells

The sleepy man of winter pulls,
Nor blows back moon-and-midnight as she blows.   30

We are the dark deniers, let us summon
Death from a summer woman,
A muscling life from lovers in their cramp,
From the fair dead who flush the sea
The bright-eyed worm on Davy's lamp,
And from the planted womb the man of straw.

We summer boys in this four-winded spinning,
Green of the seaweeds' iron,
Hold up the noisy sea and drop her birds,
Pick the world's ball of wave and froth   40
To choke the deserts with her tides,
And comb the county gardens for a wreath.

In spring we cross our foreheads with the holly,
Heigh ho the blood and berry,
And nail the merry squires to the trees;
Here love's damp muscle dries and dies,
Here break a kiss in no love's quarry.
O see the poles of promise in the boys.

III

I see you boys of summer in your ruin.
Man in his maggot's barren.   50
And boys are full and foreign in the pouch.
I am the man your father was.
We are the sons of flint and pitch.
O see the poles are kissing as they cross.

If I were tickled by the rub of love

If I were tickled by the rub of love,
A rooking girl who stole me for her side,
Broke through her straws, breaking my bandaged string,
If the red tickle as the cattle calve
Still set to scratch a laughter from my lung,
I would not fear the apple nor the flood
Nor the bad blood of spring.

Shall it be male or female? say the cells,
And drop the plum like fire from the flesh.
If I were tickled by the hatching hair,   10
The winging bone that sprouted in the heels,
The itch of man upon the baby's thigh,
I would not fear the gallows nor the axe
Nor the crossed sticks of war.

Shall it be male or female? say the fingers
That chalk the walls with green girls and their men.
I would not fear the muscling-in of love
If I were tickled by the urchin hungers
Rehearsing heat upon a raw-edged nerve.
I would not fear the devil in the loin   20
Nor the outspoken grave.

If I were tickled by the lovers' rub
That wipes away not crow's-foot nor the lock
Of sick old manhood on the fallen jaws,
Time and the crabs and the sweethearting crib
Would leave me cold as butter for the flies,
The sea of scums could drown me as it broke
Dead on the sweethearts' toes.

This world is half the devil's and my own,
Daft with the drug that's smoking in a girl   30
And curling round the bud that forks her eye.

An old man's shank one-marrowed with my bone,
And all the herrings smelling in the sea,
I sit and watch the worm beneath my nail
Wearing the quick away.

And that's the rub, the only rub that tickles.
The knobbly ape that swings along his sex
From damp love-darkness and the nurse's twist
Can never raise the midnight of a chuckle,
Nor when he finds a beauty in the breast   40
Of lover, mother, lovers, or his six
Feet in the rubbing dust.

And what's the rub? Death's feather on the nerve?
Your mouth, my love, the thistle in the kiss?
My Jack of Christ born thorny on the tree?
The words of death are dryer than his stiff,
My wordy wounds are printed with your hair.
I would be tickled by the rub that is:
Man be my metaphor.

Especially when the October wind

Especially when the October wind
With frosty fingers punishes my hair,
Caught by the crabbing sun I walk on fire
And cast a shadow crab upon the land,
By the sea's side, hearing the noise of birds,
Hearing the raven cough in winter sticks,
My busy heart who shudders as she talks
Sheds the syllabic blood and drains her words.

Shut, too, in a tower of words, I mark
On the horizon walking like the trees   10
The wordy shapes of women, and the rows
Of the star-gestured children in the park.
Some let me make you of the vowelled beeches,
Some of the oaken voices, from the roots
Of many a thorny shire tell you notes,
Some let me make you of the water's speeches.

Behind a pot of ferns the wagging clock
Tells me the hour's word, the neural meaning
Flies on the shafted disc, declaims the morning
And tells the windy weather in the cock.   20
Some let me make you of the meadow's signs;
The signal grass that tells me all I know
Breaks with the wormy winter through the eye.
Some let me tell you of the raven's sins.

Especially when the October wind
(Some let me make you of autumnal spells,
The spider-tongued, and the loud hill of Wales)
With fist of turnips punishes the land,
Some let me make you of the heartless words.
The heart is drained that, spelling in the scurry   30
Of chemic blood, warned of the coming fury.
By the sea's side hear the dark-vowelled birds.

Should lanterns shine

Should lanterns shine, the holy face,
Caught in an octagon of unaccustomed light,
Would wither up, and any boy of love
Look twice before he fell from grace.
The features in their private dark
Are formed of flesh, but let the false day come
And from her lips the faded pigments fall,
The mummy cloths expose an ancient breast.

I have been told to reason by the heart,
But heart, like head, leads helplessly;   10
I have been told to reason by the pulse,
And, when it quickens, alter the actions' pace
Till field and roof lie level and the same
So fast I move defying time, the quiet gentleman
Whose beard wags in Egyptian wind.

I have heard many years of telling,
And many years should see some change.

The ball I threw while playing in the park
Has not yet reached the ground.

Altarwise by owl-light

I

Altarwise by owl-light in the halfway-house
The gentleman lay graveward with his furies;
Abaddon in the hang-nail cracked from Adam,
And, from his fork, a dog among the fairies,
The atlas-eater with a jaw for news,
Bit out the mandrake with tomorrow's scream.
Then, penny-eyed, that gentleman of wounds,
Old cock from nowheres and the heaven's egg,
With bones unbuttoned to the halfway winds,
Hatched from the windy salvage on one leg,   10
Scraped at my cradle in a walking word
That night of time under the Christward shelter,
I am the long world's gentleman, he said,
And share my bed with Capricorn and Cancer.

IV

What is the metre of the dictionary?
The size of genesis? the short spark's gender?
Shade without shape? the shape of Pharaoh's echo?
(My shape of age nagging the wounded whisper).
Which sixth of wind blew out the burning gentry?
(Questions are hunchbacks to the poker marrow).
What of a bamboo man among your acres?
Corset the boneyards for a crooked lad?
Button your bodice on a hump of splinters,
My camel's eye will needle through the shroud.   10
Love's a reflection of the mushroom features,
Stills snapped by night in the bread-sided field,
Once close-up smiling in the wall of pictures,
Ark-lamped thrown back upon the cutting flood.

X

Let the tale's sailor from a Christian voyage
Atlaswise hold halfway off the dummy bay

Time's ship-racked gospel on the globe I balance:
So shall winged harbours through the rockbirds' eyes
Spot the blown word, and on the seas I image
December's thorn screwed in a brow of holly.
Let the first Peter from a rainbow's quayrail
Ask the tall fish swept from the bible east,
What rhubarb man peeled in her foam-blue channel
Has sown a flying garden round that sea-ghost?   10
Green as beginning, let the garden diving
Soar, with its two bark towers, to that Day
When the worm builds with the gold straws of venom
My nest of mercies in the rude, red tree.

O make me a mask

O make me a mask and a wall to shut from your spies
Of the sharp, enamelled eyes and the spectacled claws
Rape and rebellion in the nurseries of my face,
Gag of a dumbstruck tree to block from bare enemies
The bayonet tongue in this undefended prayerpiece,
The present mouth, and the sweetly blown trumpet of lies,
Shaped in old armour and oak the countenance of a dunce
To shield the glistening brain and blunt the examiners,
And a tear-stained widower grief drooped from the lashes
To veil belladonna and let the dry eyes perceive   10
Others betray the lamenting lies of their losses
By the curve of the nude mouth or the laugh up the sleeve.

Incarnate devil

Incarnate devil in a talking snake,
The central plains of Asia in his garden,
In shaping-time the circle stung awake,
In shapes of sin forked out the bearded apple,
And God walked there who was a fiddling warden
And played down pardon from the heavens' hill.

When we were strangers to the guided seas,
A handmade moon half holy in a cloud,
The wisemen tell me that the garden gods
Twined good and evil on an eastern tree;   10
And when the moon rose windily it was
Black as the beast and paler than the cross.

We in our Eden knew the secret guardian
In sacred waters that no frost could harden,
And in the mighty mornings of the earth;
Hell in a horn of sulphur and the cloven myth,
All heaven in a midnight of the sun,
A serpent fiddled in the shaping-time.

How shall my animal

How shall my animal
Whose wizard shape I trace in the cavernous skull,
Vessel of abscesses and exultation's shell,
Endure burial under the spelling wall,
The invoked, shrouding veil at the cap of the face,
Who should be furious,
Drunk as a vineyard snail, flailed like an octopus,
Roaring, crawling, quarrel
With the outside weathers,
The natural circle of the discovered skies   10
Draw down to its weird eyes?

How shall it magnetize,
Towards the studded male in a bent, midnight blaze
That melts the lionhead's heel and horseshoe of the heart,
A brute land in the cool top of the country days
To trot with a loud mate the haybeds of a mile,
Love and labour and kill
In quick, sweet, cruel light till the locked ground sprout out,
The black, burst sea rejoice,
The bowels turn turtle,   20
Claw of the crabbed veins squeeze from each red particle
The parched and raging voice?

Fishermen of mermen
Creep and harp on the tide, sinking their charmed, bent pin
With bridebait of gold bread, I with a living skein,
Tongue and ear in the thread, angle the temple-bound
Curl-locked and animal cavepools of spells and bone,
Trace out a tentacle,
Nailed with an open eye, in the bowl of wounds and weed
To clasp my fury on ground   30
And clap its great blood down;
Never shall beast be born to atlas the few seas
Or poise the day on a horn.

Sigh long, clay cold, lie shorn,
Cast high, stunned on gilled stone; sly scissors ground in frost
Clack through the thicket of strength, love hewn in pillars
    drops
With carved bird, saint, and sun, the wrackspiked maiden
    mouth
Lops, as a bush plumed with flames, the rant of the fierce eye,
Clips short the gesture of breath.
Die in red feathers when the flying heaven's cut,   40
And roll with the knocked earth:
Lie dry, rest robbed, my beast.
You have kicked from a dark den, leaped up the whinnying
    light,
And dug your grave in my breast.

After the funeral

(In memory of Ann Jones)

After the funeral, mule praises, brays,
Windshake of sailshaped ears, muffle-toed tap
Tap happily of one peg in the thick
Grave's foot, blinds down the lids, the teeth in black,
The spittled eyes, the salt ponds in the sleeves,
Morning smack of the spade that wakes up sleep,
Shakes a desolate boy who slits his throat
In the dark of the coffin and sheds dry leaves,
That breaks one bone to light with a judgment clout,
After the feast of tear-stuffed time and thistles   10
In a room with a stuffed fox and a stale fern,
I stand, for this memorial's sake, alone
In the snivelling hours with dead, humped Ann
Whose hooded, fountain heart once fell in puddles
Round the parched worlds of Wales and drowned each sun
(Though this for her is a monstrous image blindly
Magnified out of praise; her death was a still drop;
She would not have me sinking in the holy
Flood of her heart's fame; she would lie dumb and deep
And need no druid of her broken body).   20
But I, Ann's bard on a raised hearth, call all
The seas to service that her wood-tongued virtue
Babble like a bellbuoy over the hymning heads,
Bow down the walls of the ferned and foxy woods
That her love sing and swing through a brown chapel,
Bless her bent spirit with four, crossing birds.
Her flesh was meek as milk, but this skyward statue
With the wild breast and blessed and giant skull
Is carved from her in a room with a wet window
In a fiercely mourning house in a crooked year.   30
I know her scrubbed and sour humble hands
Lie with religion in their cramp, her threadbare
Whisper in a damp word, her wits drilled hollow,

Her fist of a face died clenched on a round pain;
And sculptured Ann is seventy years of stone.
These cloud-sopped, marble hands, this monumental
Argument of the hewn voice, gesture and psalm
Storm me forever over her grave until
The stuffed lung of the fox twitch and cry Love
And the strutting fern lay seeds on the black sill.   40

The tombstone told

The tombstone told when she died.
Her two surnames stopped me still.
A virgin married at rest.
She married in this pouring place,
That I struck one day by luck,
Before I heard in my mother's side
Or saw in the looking-glass shell
The rain through her cold heart speak
And the sun killed in her face.
More the thick stone cannot tell.   10

Before she lay on a stranger's bed
With a hand plunged through her hair,
Or that rainy tongue beat back
Through the devilish years and innocent deaths
To the room of a secret child,
Among men later I heard it said
She cried her white-dressed limbs were bare
And her red lips were kissed black,
She wept in her pain and made mouths,
Talked and tore though her eyes smiled.   20

I who saw in a hurried film
Death and this mad heroine
Meet once on a mortal wall
Heard her speak through the chipped beak
Of the stone bird guarding her:
I died before bedtime came
But my womb was bellowing
And I felt with my bare fall
A blazing red harsh head tear up
And the dear floods of his hair.   30

On no work of words

On no work of words now for three lean months in the bloody
Belly of the rich year and the big purse of my body
I bitterly take to task my poverty and craft:

To take to give is all, return what is hungrily given
Puffing the pounds of manna up through the dew to heaven,
The lovely gift of the gab bangs back on a blind shaft.

To lift to leave from the treasures of man is pleasing death
That will rake at last all currencies of the marked breath
And count the taken, forsaken mysteries in a bad dark.

To surrender now is to pay the expensive ogre twice.   10
Ancient woods of my blood, dash down to the nut of the seas
If I take to burn or return this world which is each man's
     work.

Twenty-four years

Twenty-four years remind the tears of my eyes.
(Bury the dead for fear that they walk to the grave in labour.)
In the groin of the natural doorway I crouched like a tailor
Sewing a shroud for a journey
By the light of the meat-eating sun.
Dressed to die, the sensual strut begun,
With my red veins full of money,
In the final direction of the elementary town
I advance for as long as forever is.

Once it was the colour of saying

Once it was the colour of saying
Soaked my table the uglier side of a hill
With a capsized field where a school sat still
And a black and white patch of girls grew playing;
The gentle seaslides of saying I must undo
That all the charmingly drowned arise to cockcrow and kill.
When I whistled with mitching boys through a reservoir park
Where at night we stoned the cold and cuckoo
Lovers in the dirt of their leafy beds,
The shade of their trees was a word of many shades   10
And a lamp of lightning for the poor in the dark;
Now my saying shall be my undoing,
And every stone I wind off like a reel.

If my head hurt a hair's foot

'If my head hurt a hair's foot
Pack back the downed bone. If the unpricked ball of my breath
Bump on a spout let the bubbles jump out.
Sooner drop with the worm of the ropes round my throat
Than bully ill love in the clouted scene.

All game phrases fit your ring of a cockfight:
I'll comb the snared woods with a glove on a lamp,
Peck, sprint, dance on fountains and duck time
Before I rush in a crouch the ghost with a hammer, air,
Strike light, and bloody a loud room.   10

If my bunched, monkey coming is cruel
Rage me back to the making house. My hand unravel
When you sew the deep door. The bed is a cross place.
Bend, if my journey ache, direction like an arc or make
A limp and riderless shape to leap nine thinning months.'

'No. Not for Christ's dazzling bed
Or a nacreous sleep among soft particles and charms
My dear would I change my tears or your iron head.
Thrust, my daughter or son, to escape, there is none, none, none,
Nor when all ponderous heaven's host of waters breaks.   20

Now to awake husked of gestures and my joy like a cave
To the anguish and carrion, to the infant forever unfree,
O my lost love bounced from a good home;
The grain that hurries this way from the rim of the grave
Has a voice and a house, and there and here you must couch and
    cry.

Rest beyond choice in the dust-appointed grain,
At the breast stored with seas. No return
Through the waves of the fat streets nor the skeleton's thin ways.
The grave and my calm body are shut to your coming as stone,
And the endless beginning of prodigies suffers open.'   30

To Others than You

Friend by enemy I call you out.

You with a bad coin in your socket,
You my friend there with a winning air
Who palmed the lie on me when you looked
Brassily at my shyest secret,
Enticed with twinkling bits of the eye
Till the sweet tooth of my love bit dry,
Rasped at last, and I stumbled and sucked,
Whom now I conjure to stand as thief
In the memory worked by mirrors,   10
With unforgettably smiling act,
Quickness of hand in the velvet glove
And my whole heart under your hammer,
Were once such a creature, so gay and frank
A desireless familiar
I never thought to utter or think
While you displaced a truth in the air,

That though I loved them for their faults
As much as for their good,
My friends were enemies on stilts   20
With their heads in a cunning cloud.

When I woke

When I woke, the town spoke.
Birds and clocks and cross bells
Dinned aside the coiling crowd,
The reptile profligates in a flame,
Spoilers and pokers of sleep,
The next-door sea dispelled
Frogs and satans and woman-luck,
While a man outside with a billhook,
Up to his head in his blood,
Cutting the morning off,   10
The warm-veined double of Time
And his scarving beard from a book,
Slashed down the last snake as though
It were a wand or subtle bough,
Its tongue peeled in the wrap of a leaf.

Every morning I make,
God in bed, good and bad,
After a water-face walk,
The death-stagged scatter-breath
Mammoth and sparrowfall   20
Everybody's earth.
Where birds ride like leaves and boats like ducks
I heard, this morning, waking,
Crossly out of the town noises
A voice in the erected air,
No prophet-progeny of mine,
Cry my sea town was breaking.
No Time, spoke the clocks, no God, rang the bells,
I drew the white sheet over the islands
And the coins on my eyelids sang like shells.   30

Paper and sticks

Paper and sticks and shovel and match
Why won't the news of the old world catch
And the fire in a temper start

Once I had a rich boy for myself
I loved his body and his navy blue wealth
And I lived in his purse and his heart

When in our bed I was tossing and turning
All I could see were his brown eyes burning
By the green of a one pound note

I talk to him as I clean the grate   10
O my dear it's never too late
To take me away as you whispered and wrote

I had a handsome and well-off boy
I'll share my money and we'll run for joy
With a bouncing and silver spooned kid

Sharp and shrill my silly tongue scratches
Words on the air as the fire catches
You never did and *he* never did.

There was a saviour

There was a saviour
Rarer than radium,
Commoner than water, crueller than truth;
Children kept from the sun
Assembled at his tongue
To hear the golden note turn in a groove,
Prisoners of wishes locked their eyes
In the jails and studies of his keyless smiles.

The voice of children says
From a lost wilderness   10
There was calm to be done in his safe unrest,
When hindering man hurt
Man, animal, or bird
We hid our fears in that murdering breath,
Silence, silence to do, when earth grew loud,
In lairs and asylums of the tremendous shout.

There was glory to hear
In the churches of his tears,
Under his downy arm you sighed as he struck,
O you who could not cry   20
On to the ground when a man died
Put a tear for joy in the unearthly flood
And laid your cheek against a cloud-formed shell:
Now in the dark there is only yourself and myself.

Two proud, blacked brothers cry,
Winter-locked side by side,
To this inhospitable hollow year,
O we who could not stir
One lean sigh when we heard
Greed on man beating near and fire neighbour   30
But wailed and nested in the sky-blue wall
Now break a giant tear for the little known fall,

      For the drooping of homes
      That did not nurse our bones,
   Brave deaths of only ones but never found,
        Now see, alone in us,
        Our own true strangers' dust
   Ride through the doors of our unentered house.
Exiled in us we arouse the soft,
Unclenched, armless, silk and rough love that breaks all rocks.   40

Deaths and Entrances

On almost the incendiary eve
   Of several near deaths,
When one at the great least of your best loved
   And always known must leave
Lions and fires of his flying breath,
   Of your immortal friends
Who'd raise the organs of the counted dust
   To shoot and sing your praise,
One who called deepest down shall hold his peace
   That cannot sink or cease   10
   Endlessly to his wound
In many married London's estranging grief.

On almost the incendiary eve
   When at your lips and keys,
Locking, unlocking, the murdered strangers weave,
   One who is most unknown,
Your polestar neighbour, sun of another street,
   Will dive up to his tears.
He'll bathe his raining blood in the male sea
   Who strode for your own dead   20
And wind his globe out of your water thread
   And load the throats of shells
   With every cry since light
Flashed first across his thunderclapping eyes.

On almost the incendiary eve
   Of deaths and entrances,
When near and strange wounded on London's waves
   Have sought your single grave,
One enemy, of many, who knows well
   Your heart is luminous   30
In the watched dark, quivering through locks and caves,
   Will pull the thunderbolts
To shut the sun, plunge, mount your darkened keys

And sear just riders back,
Until that one loved least
Looms the last Samson of your zodiac.

On the Marriage of a Virgin

Waking alone in a multitude of loves when morning's light
Surprised in the opening of her nightlong eyes
His golden yesterday asleep upon the iris
And this day's sun leapt up the sky out of her thighs
Was miraculous virginity old as loaves and fishes,
Though the moment of a miracle is unending lightning
And the shipyards of Galilee's footprints hide a navy of doves.

No longer will the vibrations of the sun desire on
Her deepsea pillow where once she married alone,
Her heart all ears and eyes, lips catching the avalanche   10
Of the golden ghost who ringed with his streams her mercury
    bone,
Who under the lids of her windows hoisted his golden luggage,
For a man sleeps where fire leapt down and she learns through
    his arm
That other sun, the jealous coursing of the unrivalled blood.

Love in the Asylum

A stranger has come
To share my room in the house not right in the head,
A girl mad as birds

Bolting the night of the door with her arm her plume.
Strait in the mazed bed
She deludes the heaven-proof house with entering clouds

Yet she deludes with walking the nightmarish room,
At large as the dead,
Or rides the imagined oceans of the male wards.

She has come possessed   10
Who admits the delusive light through the bouncing wall,
Possessed by the skies

She sleeps in the narrow trough yet she walks the dust
Yet raves at her will
On the madhouse boards worn thin by my walking tears.

And taken by light in her arms at long and dear last
I may without fail
Suffer the first vision that set fire to the stars.

The hunchback in the park

The hunchback in the park
A solitary mister
Propped between trees and water
From the opening of the garden lock
That lets the trees and water enter
Until the Sunday sombre bell at dark

Eating bread from a newspaper
Drinking water from the chained cup
That the children filled with gravel
In the fountain basin where I sailed my ship   10
Slept at night in a dog kennel
But nobody chained him up.

Like the park birds he came early
Like the water he sat down
And Mister they called Hey mister
The truant boys from the town
Running when he had heard them clearly
On out of sound.

Past lake and rockery
Laughing when he shook his paper   20
Hunchbacked in mockery
Through the loud zoo of the willow groves
Dodging the park keeper
With his stick that picked up leaves.

And the old dog sleeper
Alone between nurses and swans
While the boys among willows
Made the tigers jump out of their eyes
To roar on the rockery stones
And the groves were blue with sailors   30

Made all day until bell time
A woman figure without fault
Straight as a young elm
Straight and tall from his crooked bones
That she might stand in the night
After the locks and chains

All night in the unmade park
After the railings and shrubberies
The birds the grass the trees the lake
And the wild boys innocent as strawberries   40
Had followed the hunchback
To his kennel in the dark.

Among those killed in the Dawn Raid was a Man Aged a Hundred

When the morning was waking over the war
He put on his clothes and stepped out and he died,
The locks yawned loose and a blast blew them wide,
He dropped where he loved on the burst pavement stone
And the funeral grains of the slaughtered floor.
Tell his street on its back he stopped a sun
And the craters of his eyes grew springshoots and fire
When all the keys shot from the locks, and rang.
Dig no more for the chains of his grey-haired heart.
The heavenly ambulance drawn by a wound   10
Assembling waits for the spade's ring on the cage.
O keep his bones away from that common cart,
The morning is flying on the wings of his age
And a hundred storks perch on the sun's right hand.

Lie still, sleep becalmed

Lie still, sleep becalmed, sufferer with the wound
In the throat, burning and turning. All night afloat
On the silent sea we have heard the sound
That came from the wound wrapped in the salt sheet.

Under the mile off moon we trembled listening
To the sea sound flowing like blood from the loud wound
And when the salt sheet broke in a storm of singing
The voices of all the drowned swam on the wind.

Open a pathway through the slow sad sail,
Throw wide to the wind the gates of the wandering boat   10
For my voyage to begin to the end of my wound,
We heard the sea sound sing, we saw the salt sheet tell.
Lie still, sleep becalmed, hide the mouth in the throat,
Or we shall obey, and ride with you through the drowned.

Ceremony After a Fire Raid

I

Myselves
The grievers
Grieve
Among the street burned to tireless death
A child of a few hours
With its kneading mouth
Charred on the black breast of the grave
The mother dug, and its arms full of fires.

Begin
With singing   10
Sing
Darkness kindled back into beginning
When the caught tongue nodded blind,
A star was broken
Into the centuries of the child
Myselves grieve now, and miracles cannot atone.

Forgive
Us forgive
Give
Us your death that myselves the believers   20
May hold it in a great flood
Till the blood shall spurt,
And the dust shall sing like a bird
As the grains blow, as your death grows, through our heart.

Crying
Your dying
Cry,
Child beyond cockcrow, by the fire-dwarfed
Street we chant the flying sea
In the body bereft.   30
Love is the last light spoken. Oh
Seed of sons in the loin of the black husk left.

II

I know not whether
Adam or Eve, the adorned holy bullock
Or the white ewe lamb
Or the chosen virgin
Laid in her snow
On the altar of London,
Was the first to die
In the cinder of the little skull,   40
O bride and bride groom
O Adam and Eve together
Lying in the lull
Under the sad breast of the head stone
White as the skeleton
Of the garden of Eden.

I know the legend
Of Adam and Eve is never for a second
Silent in my service
Over the dead infants   50
Over the one
Child who was priest and servants,
Word, singers, and tongue
In the cinder of the little skull,
Who was the serpent's
Night fall and the fruit like a sun,
Man and woman undone,
Beginning crumbled back to darkness
Bare as the nurseries
Of the garden of wilderness.   60

III

Into the organpipes and steeples
Of the luminous cathedrals,
Into the weathercocks' molten mouths
Rippling in twelve-winded circles,
Into the dead clock burning the hour
Over the urn of sabbaths
Over the whirling ditch of daybreak
Over the sun's hovel and the slum of fire

And the golden pavements laid in requiems,
Into the cauldrons of the statuary, 70
Into the bread in a wheatfield of flames,
Into the wine burning like brandy,
The masses of the sea
The masses of the sea under
The masses of the infant-bearing sea
Erupt, fountain, and enter to utter for ever
Glory glory glory
The sundering ultimate kingdom of genesis' thunder.

Poem in October

It was my thirtieth year to heaven
Woke to my hearing from harbour and neighbour wood
   And the mussel pooled and the heron
         Priested shore
         The morning beckon
With water praying and call of seagull and rook
And the knock of sailing boats on the net webbed wall
     Myself to set foot
       That second
In the still sleeping town and set forth.   10

My birthday began with the water-
Birds and the birds of the winged trees flying my name
   Above the farms and the white horses
        And I rose
       In rainy autumn
And walked abroad in a shower of all my days.
High tide and the heron dived when I took the road
     Over the border
       And the gates
Of the town closed as the town awoke.   20

   A springful of larks in a rolling
Cloud and the roadside bushes brimming with whistling
   Blackbirds and the sun of October
        Summery
       On the hill's shoulder,
Here were fond climates and sweet singers suddenly
Come in the morning where I wandered and listened
     To the rain wringing
       Wind blow cold
In the wood faraway under me.   30

   Pale rain over the dwindling harbour
And over the sea wet church the size of a snail

With its horns through mist and the castle
            Brown as owls
        But all the gardens
Of spring and summer were blooming in the tall tales
Beyond the border and under the lark full cloud.
            There could I marvel
                My birthday
Away but the weather turned around.   40

It turned away from the blithe country
And down the other air and the blue altered sky
    Streamed again a wonder of summer
                With apples
            Pears and red currants
And I saw in the turning so clearly a child's
Forgotten mornings when he walked with his mother
            Through the parables
                Of sun light
And the legends of the green chapels   50

And the twice told fields of infancy
That his tears burned my cheeks and his heart moved in mine.
    These were the woods the river and sea
                Where a boy
            In the listening
Summertime of the dead whispered the truth of his joy
To the trees and the stones and the fish in the tide.
            And the mystery
                Sang alive
Still in the water and singingbirds.   60

And there could I marvel my birthday
Away but the weather turned around. And the true
    Joy of the long dead child sang burning
                In the sun.
        It was my thirtieth
Year to heaven stood there then in the summer noon
Though the town below lay leaved with October blood.

O may my heart's truth
Still be sung
On this high hill in a year's turning.　　70

Holy Spring

O
Out of a bed of love
When that immortal hospital made one more move to soothe
The cureless counted body,
And ruin and his causes
Over the barbed and shooting sea assumed an army
And swept into our wounds and houses,
I climb to greet the war in which I have no heart but only
That one dark I owe my light,
Call for confessor and wiser mirror but there is none   10
To glow after the god stoning night
And I am struck as lonely as a holy maker by the sun.

No
Praise that the spring time is all
Gabriel and radiant shrubbery as the morning grows joyful
Out of the woebegone pyre
And the multitude's sultry tear turns cool on the weeping wall,
My arising prodigal
Sun the father his quiver full of the infants of pure fire,
But blessed be hail and upheaval   20
That uncalm still it is sure alone to stand and sing
Alone in the husk of man's home
And the mother and toppling house of the holy spring;
If only for a last time.

The conversation of prayers

The conversation of prayers about to be said
By the child going to bed and the man on the stairs
Who climbs to his dying love in her high room,
The one not caring to whom in his sleep he will move
And the other full of tears that she will be dead,

Turns in the dark on the sound they know will arise
Into the answering skies from the green ground,
From the man on the stairs and the child by his bed.
The sound about to be said in the two prayers
For the sleep in a safe land and the love who dies   10

Will be the same grief flying. Whom shall they calm?
Shall the child sleep unharmed or the man be crying?
The conversation of prayers about to be said
Turns on the quick and the dead, and the man on the stairs
Tonight shall find no dying but alive and warm

In the fire of his care his love in the high room.
And the child not caring to whom he climbs his prayer
Shall drown in a grief as deep as his true grave,
And mark the dark eyed wave, through the eyes of sleep,
Dragging him up the stairs to one who lies dead.   20

A Refusal to Mourn the Death, by Fire, of a Child in London

Never until the mankind making
Bird beast and flower
Fathering and all humbling darkness
Tells with silence the last light breaking
And the still hour
Is come of the sea tumbling in harness

And I must enter again the round
Zion of the water bead
And the synagogue of the ear of corn
Shall I let pray the shadow of a sound   10
Or sow my salt seed
In the least valley of sackcloth to mourn

The majesty and burning of the child's death.
I shall not murder
The mankind of her going with a grave truth
Nor blaspheme down the stations of the breath
With any further
Elegy of innocence and youth.

Deep with the first dead lies London's daughter,
Robed in the long friends,   20
The grains beyond age, the dark veins of her mother,
Secret by the unmourning water
Of the riding Thames.
After the first death, there is no other.

This side of the truth

(for Llewelyn)

This side of the truth,
You may not see, my son.
King of your blue eyes
In the blinding country of youth,
That all is undone,
Under the unminding skies,
Of innocence and guilt
Before you move to make
One gesture of the heart or head,
Is gathered and spilt   10
Into the winding dark
Like the dust of the dead.

Good and bad, two ways
Of moving about your death
By the grinding sea,
King of your heart in the blind days,
Blow away like breath,
Go crying through you and me
And the souls of all men
Into the innocent   20
Dark, and the guilty dark, and good
Death, and bad death, and then
In the last element
Fly like the stars' blood,

Like the sun's tears,
Like the moon's seed, rubbish
And fire, the flying rant
Of the sky, king of your six years.
And the wicked wish,
Down the beginning of plants   30
And animals and birds,

Water and light, the earth and sky,
Is cast before you move,
And all your deeds and words,
Each truth, each lie,
Die in unjudging love.

A Winter's Tale

It is a winter's tale
That the snow blind twilight ferries over the lakes
And floating fields from the farm in the cup of the vales,
Gliding windless through the hand folded flakes,
The pale breath of cattle at the stealthy sail,

And the stars falling cold,
And the smell of hay in the snow, and the far owl
Warning among the folds, and the frozen hold
Flocked with the sheep white smoke of the farm house cowl
In the river wended vales where the tale was told.   10

Once when the world turned old
On a star of faith pure as the drifting bread,
As the food and flames of the snow, a man unrolled
The scrolls of fire that burned in his heart and head,
Torn and alone in a farm house in a fold

Of fields. And burning then
In his firelit island ringed by the winged snow
And the dung hills white as wool and the hen
Roosts sleeping chill till the flame of the cock crow
Combs through the mantled yards and the morning men   20

Stumble out with their spades,
The cattle stirring, the mousing cat stepping shy,
The puffed birds hopping and hunting, the milk maids
Gentle in their clogs over the fallen sky,
And all the woken farm at its white trades,

He knelt, he wept, he prayed,
By the spit and the black pot in the log bright light
And the cup and the cut bread in the dancing shade,

In the muffled house, in the quick of night,
At the point of love, forsaken and afraid. 30

    He knelt on the cold stones,
He wept from the crest of grief, he prayed to the veiled sky
May his hunger go howling on bare white bones
Past the statues of the stables and the sky roofed sties
And the duck pond glass and the blinding byres alone

    Into the home of prayers
And fires where he should prowl down the cloud
Of his snow blind love and rush in the white lairs.
His naked need struck him howling and bowed
Though no sound flowed down the hand folded air 40

    But only the wind strung
Hunger of birds in the fields of the bread of water, tossed
In high corn and the harvest melting on their tongues.
And his nameless need bound him burning and lost
When cold as snow he should run the wended vales among

    The rivers mouthed in night,
And drown in the drifts of his need, and lie curled caught
In the always desiring centre of the white
Inhuman cradle and the bride bed forever sought
By the believer lost and the hurled outcast of light. 50

    Deliver him, he cried,
By losing him all in love, and cast his need
Alone and naked in the engulfing bride,
Never to flourish in the fields of the white seed
Or flower under the time dying flesh astride.

    Listen. The minstrels sing
In the departed villages. The nightingale,
Dust in the buried wood, flies on the grains of her wings
And spells on the winds of the dead his winter's tale.
The voice of the dust of water from the withered spring 60

    Is telling. The wizened
Stream with bells and baying water bounds. The dew rings

On the gristed leaves and the long gone glistening
Parish of snow. The carved mouths in the rock are wind swept
    strings.
Time sings through the intricately dead snow drop. Listen.

      It was a hand or sound
In the long ago land that glided the dark door wide
And there outside on the bread of the ground
A she bird rose and rayed like a burning bride.
A she bird dawned, and her breast with snow and scarlet
    downed.   70

      Look. And the dancers move
On the departed, snow bushed green, wanton in moon light
As a dust of pigeons. Exulting, the grave hooved
Horses, centaur dead, turn and tread the drenched white
Paddocks in the farms of birds. The dead oak walks for love.

      The carved limbs in the rock
Leap, as to trumpets. Calligraphy of the old
Leaves is dancing. Lines of age on the stones weave in a flock.
And the harp shaped voice of the water's dust plucks in a fold
Of fields. For love, the long ago she bird rises. Look.   80

      And the wild wings were raised
Above her folded head, and the soft feathered voice
Was flying through the house as though the she bird praised
And all the elements of the slow fall rejoiced
That a man knelt alone in the cup of the vales,

      In the mantle and calm,
By the spit and the black pot in the log bright light.
And the sky of birds in the plumed voice charmed
Him up and he ran like a wind after the kindling flight
Past the blind barns and byres of the windless farm.   90

      In the poles of the year
When black birds died like priests in the cloaked hedge row
And over the cloth of counties the far hills rode near,

Under the one leaved trees ran a scarecrow of snow
And fast through the drifts of the thickets antlered like deer,

    Rags and prayers down the knee-
Deep hillocks and loud on the numbed lakes,
All night lost and long wading in the wake of the she-
Bird through the times and lands and tribes of the slow flakes.
Listen and look where she sails the goose plucked sea,   100

    The sky, the bird, the bride,
The cloud, the need, the planted stars, the joy beyond
The fields of seed and the time dying flesh astride,
The heavens, the heaven, the grave, the burning font.
In the far ago land the door of his death glided wide,

    And the bird descended.
On a bread white hill over the cupped farm
And the lakes and floating fields and the river wended
Vales where he prayed to come to the last harm
And the home of prayers and fires, the tale ended.   110

    The dancing perishes
On the white, no longer growing green, and, minstrel dead,
The singing breaks in the snow shoed villages of wishes
That once cut the figures of birds on the deep bread
And over the glazed lakes skated the shapes of fishes

    Flying. The rite is shorn
Of nightingale and centaur dead horse. The springs wither
Back. Lines of age sleep on the stones till trumpeting dawn.
Exultation lies down. Time buries the spring weather
That belled and bounded with the fossil and the dew reborn.   120

    For the bird lay bedded
In a choir of wings, as though she slept or died,
And the wings glided wide and he was hymned and wedded,
And through the thighs of the engulfing bride,
The woman breasted and the heaven headed

    Bird, he was brought low,
Burning in the bride bed of love, in the whirl-

Pool at the wanting centre, in the folds
Of paradise, in the spun bud of the world.
And she rose with him flowering in her melting snow.   130

In my craft or sullen art

In my craft or sullen art
Exercised in the still night
When only the moon rages
And the lovers lie abed
With all their griefs in their arms,
I labour by singing light
Not for ambition or bread
Or the strut and trade of charms
On the ivory stages
But for the common wages   10
Of their most secret heart.

Not for the proud man apart
From the raging moon I write
On these spindrift pages
Nor for the towering dead
With their nightingales and psalms
But for the lovers, their arms
Round the griefs of the ages,
Who pay no praise or wages
Nor heed my craft or art.   20

Fern Hill

Now as I was young and easy under the apple boughs
About the lilting house and happy as the grass was green.
  The night above the dingle starry,
   Time let me hail and climb
  Golden in the heydays of his eyes,
And honoured among wagons I was prince of the apple towns
And once below a time I lordly had the trees and leaves
   Trail with daisies and barley
  Down the rivers of the windfall light.

And as I was green and carefree, famous among the barns 10
About the happy yard and singing as the farm was home,
  In the sun that is young once only,
   Time let me play and be
  Golden in the mercy of his means,
And green and golden I was huntsman and herdsman, the calves
Sang to my horn, the foxes on the hills barked clear and cold,
   And the sabbath rang slowly
  In the pebbles of the holy streams.

All the sun long it was running, it was lovely, the hay
Fields high as the house, the tunes from the chimneys,
 it was air 20
  And playing, lovely and watery
   And fire green as grass.
  And nightly under the simple stars
As I rode to sleep the owls were bearing the farm away,
All the moon long I heard, blessed among stables, the nightjars
  Flying with the ricks, and the horses
   Flashing into the dark.

And then to awake, and the farm, like a wanderer white
With the dew, come back, the cock on his shoulder: it was all
  Shining, it was Adam and maiden, 30
   The sky gathered again
  And the sun grew round that very day.

So it must have been after the birth of the simple light
In the first, spinning place, the spellbound horses walking warm
    Out of the whinnying green stable
        On to the fields of praise.

And honoured among foxes and pheasants by the gay house
Under the new made clouds and happy as the heart was long,
    In the sun born over and over,
        I ran my heedless ways,   40
    My wishes raced through the house high hay
And nothing I cared, at my sky blue trades, that time allows
In all his tuneful turning so few and such morning songs
    Before the children green and golden
        Follow him out of grace,

Nothing I cared, in the lamb white days, that time would take me
Up to the swallow thronged loft by the shadow of my hand,
    In the moon that is always rising,
        Nor that riding to sleep
    I should hear him fly with the high fields   50
And wake to the farm forever fled from the childless land.
Oh as I was young and easy in the mercy of his means,
        Time held me green and dying
        Though I sang in my chains like the sea.

On a Wedding Anniversary

The sky is torn across
This ragged anniversary of two
Who moved for three years in tune
Down the long walks of their vows.

Now their love lies a loss
And Love and his patients roar on a chain;
From every true or crater
Carrying cloud, Death strikes their house.

Too late in the wrong rain
They come together whom their love parted: 10
The windows pour into their heart
And the doors burn in their brain.

In Country Sleep

I

Never and never, my girl riding far and near
In the land of the hearthstone tales, and spelled asleep,
Fear or believe that the wolf in a sheepwhite hood
Loping and bleating roughly and blithely shall leap,
                    My dear, my dear,
Out of a lair in the flocked leaves in the dew dipped year
To eat your heart in the house in the rosy wood.

Sleep, good, for ever, slow and deep, spelled rare and wise,
My girl ranging the night in the rose and shire
Of the hobnail tales: no gooseherd or swine will turn   10
Into a homestall king or hamlet of fire
                    And prince of ice
To court the honeyed heart from your side before sunrise
In a spinney of ringed boys and ganders, spike and burn,

Nor the innocent lie in the rooting dingle wooed
And staved, and riven among plumes my rider weep.
From the broomed witch's spume you are shielded by fern
And flower of country sleep and the greenwood keep.
                    Lie fast and soothed,
Safe be and smooth from the bellows of the rushy brood.   20
Never, my girl, until tolled to sleep by the stern

Bell believe or fear that the rustic shade or spell
Shall harrow and snow the blood while you ride wide and near,
For who unmanningly haunts the mountain ravened eaves
Or skulks in the dell moon but moonshine echoing clear
                    From the starred well?
A hill touches an angel. Out of a saint's cell
The nightbird lauds through nunneries and domes of leaves

Her robin breasted tree, three Marys in the rays.
Sanctum sanctorum the animal eye of the wood   30
In the rain telling its beads, and the gravest ghost
The owl at its knelling. Fox and holt kneel before blood.

Now the tales praise
The star rise at pasture and nightlong the fables graze
On the lord's table of the bowing grass. Fear most

For ever of all not the wolf in his baaing hood
Nor the tusked prince, in the ruttish farm, at the rind
And mire of love, but the Thief as meek as the dew.
The country is holy: O bide in that country kind,
                    Know the green good,   40
Under the prayer wheeling moon in the rosy wood
Be shielded by chant and flower and gay may you

Lie in grace. Sleep spelled at rest in the lowly house
In the squirrel nimble grove, under linen and thatch
And star: held and blessed, though you scour the high four
Winds, from the dousing shade and the roarer at the latch,
                    Cool in your vows.
Yet out of the beaked, web dark and the pouncing boughs
Be you sure the Thief will seek a way sly and sure

And sly as snow and meek as dew blown to the thorn,   50
This night and each vast night until the stern bell talks
In the tower and tolls to sleep over the stalls
Of the hearthstone tales my own, last love; and the soul walks
                    The waters shorn.
This night and each night since the falling star you were born,
Ever and ever he finds a way, as the snow falls,

As the rain falls, hail on the fleece, as the vale mist rides
Through the haygold stalls, as the dew falls on the wind-
Milled dust of the apple tree and the pounded islands
Of the morning leaves, as the star falls, as the winged   60
                    Apple seed glides,
And falls, and flowers in the yawning wound at our sides,
As the world falls, silent as the cyclone of silence.

II
Night and the reindeer on the clouds above the haycocks
And the wings of the great roc ribboned for the fair!
The leaping saga of prayer! And high, there, on the hare-

Heeled winds the rooks
Cawing from their black bethels soaring, the holy books
Of birds! Among the cocks like fire the red fox

Burning! Night and the vein of birds in the winged, sloe wrist   70
Of the wood! Pastoral beat of blood through the laced leaves!
The stream from the priest black wristed spinney and sleeves
Of thistling frost
Of the nightingale's din and tale! The upgiven ghost
Of the dingle torn to singing and the surpliced

Hill of cypresses! The din and tale in the skimmed
Yard of the buttermilk rain on the pail! The sermon
Of blood! The bird loud vein! The saga from mermen
To seraphim
Leaping! The gospel rooks! All tell, this night, of him   80
Who comes as red as the fox and sly as the heeled wind.

Illumination of music! the lulled black backed
Gull, on the wave with sand in its eyes! And the foal moves
Through the shaken greensward lake, silent, on moonshod
hooves,
In the winds' wakes.
Music of elements, that a miracle makes!
Earth, air, water, fire, singing into the white act,

The haygold haired, my love asleep, and the rift blue
Eyed, in the haloed house, in her rareness and hilly
High riding, held and blessed and true, and so stilly   90
Lying the sky
Might cross its planets, the bell weep, night gather her eyes,
The Thief fall on the dead like the willynilly dew,

Only for the turning of the earth in her holy
Heart! Slyly, slowly, hearing the wound in her side go
Round the sun, he comes to my love like the designed snow,
And truly he
Flows to the strand of flowers like the dew's ruly sea,
And surely he sails like the ship shape clouds. Oh he

Comes designed to my love to steal not her tide raking   100
Wound, nor her riding high, nor her eyes, nor kindled hair,
But her faith that each vast night and the saga of prayer
                    He comes to take
Her faith that this last night for his unsacred sake
He comes to leave her in the lawless sun awaking

Naked and forsaken to grieve he will not come.
Ever and ever by all your vows believe and fear
My dear this night he comes and night without end my dear
                    Since you were born:
And you shall wake, from country sleep, this dawn and each first
    dawn,   110
Your faith as deathless as the outcry of the ruled sun.

Over Sir John's hill

Over Sir John's hill,
The hawk on fire hangs still;
In a hoisted cloud, at drop of dusk, he pulls to his claws
And gallows, up the rays of his eyes the small birds of the bay
And the shrill child's play
Wars
Of the sparrows and such who swansing, dusk, in wrangling
 hedges.
And blithely they squawk
To fiery tyburn over the wrestle of elms until
The flash the noosed hawk   10
Crashes, and slowly the fishing holy stalking heron
In the river Towy below bows his tilted headstone.

Flash, and the plumes crack,
And a black cap of jack-
Daws Sir John's just hill dons, and again the gulled birds hare
To the hawk on fire, the halter height, over Towy's fins,
In a whack of wind.
There
Where the elegiac fisherbird stabs and paddles
In the pebbly dab filled   20
Shallow and sedge, and 'dilly dilly,' calls the loft hawk,
'Come and be killed,'
I open the leaves of the water at a passage
Of psalms and shadows among the pincered sandcrabs prancing

And read, in a shell,
Death clear as a buoy's bell:
All praise of the hawk on fire in hawk-eyed dusk be sung,
When his viperish fuse hangs looped with flames under the brand
Wing, and blest shall
Young   30
Green chickens of the bay and bushes cluck, 'dilly dilly,
Come let us die.'

We grieve as the blithe birds, never again, leave shingle and elm,
The heron and I,
I young Aesop fabling to the near night by the dingle
Of eels, saint heron hymning in the shell-hung distant

Crystal harbour vale
Where the sea cobbles sail,
And wharves of water where the walls dance and the white
    cranes stilt.
It is the heron and I, under judging Sir John's elmed   40
Hill, tell-tale the knelled
Guilt
Of the led-astray birds whom God, for their breast of whistles,
Have mercy on,
God in his whirlwind silence save, who marks the sparrows hail,
For their souls' song.
Now the heron grieves in the weeded verge. Through windows
Of dusk and water I see the tilting whispering

Heron, mirrored, go,
As the snapt feathers snow,   50
Fishing in the tear of the Towy. Only a hoot owl
Hollows, a grassblade blown in cupped hands, in the looted elms,
And no green cocks or hens
Shout
Now on Sir John's hill. The heron, ankling the scaly
Lowlands of the waves,
Makes all the music; and I who hear the tune of the slow,
Wear-willow river, grave,
Before the lunge of the night, the notes on this time-shaken
Stone for the sake of the souls of the slain birds sailing.   60

In the White Giant's Thigh

Through throats where many rivers meet, the curlews cry,
Under the conceiving moon, on the high chalk hill,
And there this night I walk in the white giant's thigh
Where barren as boulders women lie longing still

To labour and love though they lay down long ago.

Through throats where many rivers meet, the women pray,
Pleading in the waded bay for the seed to flow
Though the names on their weed grown stones are rained away,

And alone in the night's eternal, curving act
They yearn with tongues of curlews for the unconceived   10
And immemorial sons of the cudgelling, hacked

Hill. Who once in gooseskin winter loved all ice leaved
In the courters' lanes, or twined in the ox roasting sun
In the wains tonned so high that the wisps of the hay
Clung to the pitching clouds, or gay with anyone
Young as they in the after milking moonlight lay

Under the lighted shapes of faith and their moonshade
Petticoats galed high, or shy with the rough riding boys,
Now clasp me to their grains in the gigantic glade,

Who once, green countries since, were a hedgerow of joys.   20

Time by, their dust was flesh the swineherd rooted sly,
Flared in the reek of the wiving sty with the rush
Light of his thighs, spreadeagle to the dunghill sky,
Or with their orchard man in the core of the sun's bush
Rough as cows' tongues and thrashed with brambles their
    buttermilk
Manes, under his quenchless summer barbed gold to the bone,

Or rippling soft in the spinney moon as the silk
And ducked and draked white lake that harps to a hail stone.

Who once were a bloom of wayside brides in the hawed house
And heard the lewd, wooed field flow to the coming frost,   30
The scurrying, furred small friars squeal, in the dowse
Of day, in the thistle aisles, till the white owl crossed

Their breast, the vaulting does roister, the horned bucks climb
Quick in the wood at love, where a torch of foxes foams,
All birds and beasts of the linked night uproar and chime

And the mole snout blunt under his pilgrimage of domes,

Or, butter fat goosegirls, bounced in a gambo bed,
Their breasts full of honey, under their gander king
Trounced by his wings in the hissing shippen, long dead
And gone that barley dark where their clogs danced in the
    spring,   40
And their firefly hairpins flew, and the ricks ran round –

(But nothing bore, no mouthing babe to the veined hives
Hugged, and barren and bare on Mother Goose's ground
They with the simple Jacks were a boulder of wives) –

Now curlew cry me down to kiss the mouths of their dust.

The dust of their kettles and clocks swings to and fro
Where the hay rides now or the bracken kitchens rust
As the arc of the billhooks that flashed the hedges low
And cut the birds' boughs that the minstrel sap ran red.
They from houses where the harvest kneels, hold me hard,   50
Who heard the tall bell sail down the Sundays of the dead
And the rain wring out its tongues on the faded yard,
Teach me the love that is evergreen after the fall leaved
Grave, after Beloved on the grass gulfed cross is scrubbed
Off by the sun and Daughters no longer grieved
Save by their long desirers in the fox cubbed
Streets or hungering in the crumbled wood: to these

Hale dead and deathless do the women of the hill
Love forever meridian through the courters' trees

And the daughters of darkness flame like Fawkes fires still. 60

Lament

When I was a windy boy and a bit
And the black spit of the chapel fold,
(Sighed the old ram rod, dying of women),
I tiptoed shy in the gooseberry wood,
The rude owl cried like a telltale tit,
I skipped in a blush as the big girls rolled
Ninepin down on the donkeys' common,
And on seesaw sunday nights I wooed
Whoever I would with my wicked eyes,
The whole of the moon I could love and leave   10
All the green leaved little weddings' wives
In the coal black bush and let them grieve.

When I was a gusty man and a half
And the black beast of the beetles' pews,
(Sighed the old ram rod, dying of bitches),
Not a boy and a bit in the wick-
Dipping moon and drunk as a new dropped calf,
I whistled all night in the twisted flues,
Midwives grew in the midnight ditches,
And the sizzling beds of the town cried, Quick! –   20
Whenever I dove in a breast high shoal,
Wherever I ramped in the clover quilts,
Whatsoever I did in the coal-
Black night, I left my quivering prints.

When I was a man you could call a man
And the black cross of the holy house,
(Sighed the old ram rod, dying of welcome),
Brandy and ripe in my bright, bass prime,
No springtailed tom in the red hot town
With every simmering woman his mouse   30
But a hillocky bull in the swelter
Of summer come in his great good time
To the sultry, biding herds, I said,
Oh, time enough when the blood creeps cold,

And I lie down but to sleep in bed,
For my sulking, skulking, coal black soul!

When I was a half of the man I was
And serve me right as the preachers warn,
(Sighed the old ram rod, dying of downfall),
No flailing calf or cat in a flame   40
Or hickory bull in milky grass
But a black sheep with a crumpled horn,
At last the soul from its foul mousehole
Slunk pouting out when the limp time came;
And I gave my soul a blind, slashed eye,
Gristle and rind, and a roarer's life,
And I shoved it into the coal black sky
To find a woman's soul for a wife.

Now I am a man no more no more
And a black reward for a roaring life,   50
(Sighed the old ram rod, dying of strangers),
Tidy and cursed in my dove cooed room
I lie down thin and hear the good bells jaw –
For, oh, my soul found a sunday wife
In the coal black sky and she bore angels!
Harpies around me out of her womb!
Chastity prays for me, piety sings,
Innocence sweetens my last black breath,
Modesty hides my thighs in her wings,
And all the deadly virtues plague my death!   60

Eli Jenkins's hymn to
the morning, from **Under Milk Wood**

Dear Gwalia! I know there are
Towns lovelier than ours,
And fairer hills and loftier far,
And groves more full of flowers,

And boskier woods more blithe with spring
And bright with birds' adorning,
And sweeter bards than I to sing
Their praise this beauteous morning.

By Cader Idris, tempest-torn,
Or Moel y Wyddfa's glory,   10
Carnedd Llewelyn beauty born,
Plinlimmon old in story,

By mountains where King Arthur dreams,
By Penmaen Mawr defiant,
Llareggub Hill a molehill seems,
A pygmy to a giant.

By Sawdde, Senni, Dovey, Dee,
Edw, Eden, Aled, all,
Taff and Towy broad and free,
Llyfnant with its waterfall,   20

Claerwen, Cleddau, Dulas, Daw,
Ely, Gwili, Ogwr, Nedd,
Small is our *River Dewi*, Lord,
A baby on a rushy bed.

By Carreg Cennen, King of time,
Our *Heron Head* is only

A bit of stone with seaweed spread
Where gulls come to be lonely.

A tiny dingle is *Milk Wood*
By golden Grove 'neath Grongar,   30
But let me choose and oh! I should
Love all my life and longer

To stroll among our trees and stray
In Goosegog Lane, on Donkey Down,
And hear the Dewi sing all day,
And never, never leave the town.

Do not go gentle into that good night

Do not go gentle into that good night,
Old age should burn and rave at close of day;
Rage, rage against the dying of the light.

Though wise men at their end know dark is right,
Because their words had forked no lightning they
Do not go gentle into that good night.

Good men, the last wave by, crying how bright
Their frail deeds might have danced in a green bay,
Rage, rage against the dying of the light.

Wild men who caught and sang the sun in flight,   10
And learn, too late, they grieved it on its way,
Do not go gentle into that good night.

Grave men, near death, who see with blinding sight
Blind eyes could blaze like meteors and be gay,
Rage, rage against the dying of the light.

And you, my father, there on the sad height,
Curse, bless, me now with your fierce tears, I pray.
Do not go gentle into that good night.
Rage, rage against the dying of the light.

Poem on his Birthday

In the mustardseed sun,
By full tilt river and switchback sea
    Where the cormorants scud,
In his house on stilts high among beaks
    And palavers of birds
This sandgrain day in the bent bay's grave
    He celebrates and spurns
His driftwood thirty-fifth wind turned age;
    Herons spire and spear.

Under and round him go   10
Flounders, gulls, on their cold, dying trails,
    Doing what they are told,
Curlews aloud in the congered waves
    Work at their ways to death,
And the rhymer in the long tongued room,
    Who tolls his birthday bell,
Toils towards the ambush of his wounds;
    Herons, steeple stemmed, bless.

In the thistledown fall,
He sings towards anguish; finches fly   20
    In the claw tracks of hawks
On a seizing sky; small fishes glide
    Through wynds and shells of drowned
Ships towns to pastures of otters. He
    In his slant, racking house
And the hewn coils of his trade perceives
    Herons walk in their shroud.

The livelong river's robe
Of minnows wreathing around their prayer;
    And far at sea he knows,   30
Who slaves to his crouched, eternal end
    Under a serpent cloud,

Dolphins dive in their turnturtle dust,
    The rippled seals streak down
To kill and their own tide daubing blood
    Slides good in the sleek mouth.

    In a cavernous, swung
Wave's silence, wept white angelus knells.
    Thirty-five bells sing struck
On skull and scar where his loves lie wrecked,   40
    Steered by the falling stars.
And tomorrow weeps in a blind cage
    Terror will rage apart
Before chains break to a hammer flame
    And love unbolts the dark

    And freely he goes lost
In the unknown, famous light of great
    And fabulous, dear God.
Dark is a way and light is a place,
    Heaven that never was   50
Nor will be ever is always true,
    And, in that brambled void,
Plenty as blackberries in the woods
    The dead grow for His joy.

    There he might wander bare
With the spirits of the horseshoe bay
    Or the stars' seashore dead,
Marrow of eagles, the roots of whales
    And wishbones of wild geese,
With blessed, unborn God and His Ghost,   60
    And every soul His priest,
Gulled and chanter in young Heaven's fold
    Be at cloud quaking peace,

    But dark is a long way.
He, on the earth of the night, alone
    With all the living, prays,
Who knows the rocketing wind will blow
    The bones out of the hills,

And the scythed boulders bleed, and the last
   Rage shattered waters kick   70
Masts and fishes to the still quick stars,
   Faithlessly unto Him

   Who is the light of old
And air shaped Heaven where souls grow wild
   As horses in the foam:
Oh, let me midlife mourn by the shrined
   And druid herons' vows
The voyage to ruin I must run,
   Dawn ships clouted aground,
Yet, though I cry with tumbledown tongue,   80
   Count my blessings aloud:

   Four elements and five
Senses, and man a spirit in love
   Tangling through this spun slime
To his nimbus bell cool kingdom come
   And the lost, moonshine domes,
And the sea that hides his secret selves
   Deep in its black, base bones,
Lulling of spheres in the seashell flesh,
   And this last blessing most,   90

   That the closer I move
To death, one man through his sundered hulks,
   The louder the sun blooms
And the tusked, ramshackling sea exults;
   And every wave of the way
And gale I tackle, the whole world then
   With more triumphant faith
Than ever was since the world was said
   Spins its morning of praise,

   I hear the bouncing hills   100
Grow larked and greener at berry brown
   Fall and the dew larks sing
Taller this thunderclap spring, and how
   More spanned with angels ride

The mansouled fiery islands! Oh,
  Holier then their eyes,
And my shining men no more alone
  As I sail out to die.

Elegy

Too proud to die, broken and blind he died
The darkest way, and did not turn away,
A cold, kind man brave in his burning pride

On that darkest day. Oh, forever may
He live lightly, at last, on the last, crossed
Hill, and there grow young, under the grass, in love,

Among the long flocks, and never lie lost
Or still all the days of his death, though above
All he longed all dark for his mother's breast

Which was rest and dust, and in the kind ground   10
The darkest justice of death, blind and unblessed.
Let him find no rest but be fathered and found,

I prayed in the crouching room, by his blind bed,
In the muted house, one minute before
Noon, and night, and light. The rivers of the dead

Moved in his poor hand I held, and I saw
Through his faded eyes to the roots of the sea.
Go calm to your crucifixed hill, I told

The air that drew away from him.

Notes

Comments from the poet's letters are quoted from *The Collected Letters*, ed. Paul Ferris (London: Dent, 1985)

p. 3 *Prologue*: (August 1952) Written specially for *Collected Poems, 1952*. 'I hope the Prologue *does* read as a prologue, and not as just another poem. I think – though I am too near it now to be any judge – that it *does* do what it sets out to do: addresses the readers, the "strangers", with a flourish, and fanfare, and makes clear, or tries to make clear, the position of one writer in a world "at poor peace" ' (letter to E. F. Bozman, 10 September 1952). The Prologue ('This rumpus of shapes', l. 37) dedicates the *Collected Poems* ('these seathumbed leaves', l. 29). The first and last lines rhyme, and so on inwards until the exact centre of the poem (ll. 51, 52) is a rhyming couplet.

p. 6 *The spire cranes*: (*Notebook* version January 1931) The spire is a metaphor for the poet. The stone birds carved in its masonry represent those poems which, because they are either too artificially made or too private in their meaning, fail to escape into communication with the outside world. In contrast, the chimes and the real living birds suggest a more vital and communicating kind of poetry, because they do escape from the poet-spire.

p. 7 *Out of the sighs*: (*Notebook* version June–July 1932) As a first entry into this poem the reader would do well to hold quite literally to the idea of disappointment in love; but it will also be seen that the poem registers a disaffection with life in general. The poem advocates a stoic realism regarding life's small rewards: 'Crumbs, barn, and halter' (l. 30).

p. 8 *I have longed to move away*: (*Notebook* version March 1933) The speaker wishes to escape from social and religious conventions, which he considers bogus and hypocritical. But the thought worries him (ll. 11–14) that what he now regards as dead convention might still burst into life, leaving him stranded and vulnerable to more serious terrors.

p. 9 *And death shall have no dominion*: (*Notebook* version April 1933)

The repeated first line is based on a verse in St Paul's Epistle to the Romans (6:9): 'Christ being raised from the dead dieth no more; death hath no more dominion over him.' And ll.7 and 11–12 suggest Revelation 20:13: 'And the sea gave up the dead which were in it'. But Thomas's poem is more pantheistic than Christian. It affirms the indissolubility of the general fact and principle of life, not any promise of individual Christian resurrection.

p. 10 *We lying by seasand*: (*Notebook* version May 1933) 'I often go down in the mornings to the furthest point of Gower – the village of Rhosssilli – and stay there until evening. The bay is the wildest, bleakest, and barrennest I know – four or five miles of yellow coldness going away into the distance of the sea. And the Worm* [*In the margin*: *Perhaps this accounts for my Complex], a seaworm of rock pointing into the channel, is the very promontory of depression . . . There is one table of rock on the Worm's back that is covered with long yellow grass' (letter to Pamela Hansford Johnson, probably early December 1933).

p. 11 *Here in this spring:* (*Notebook* version July 1933)

p. 12 *Ears in the turrets hear*: (*Notebook* version July 1933) 'And living in your own private, four-walled world as exclusively as possible isn't escapism, I'm sure; it isn't the Ivory Tower, and, even if it were, you secluded in your Tower know and learn more of the world outside than the outside-man who is mixed up so personally and inextricably with the mud and the unlovely people – (sorry, old Christian) – and the four bloody muddy winds' (letter to Vernon Watkins, 20 April 1936). The poem is about the self-absorption of Thomas the man and the private nature of his poetic world. It shows his fear and uncertainty in recognizing, in Donne's words, that 'No man is an island unto himself.'

p. 14 *Why east wind chills*: (*Notebook* version July 1933) The theme is man's necessary ignorance of any final answers in the face of a mysterious universe. The basic futility of the questions in the opening lines makes fun of our tendency to seek intellectual explanations of natural mysteries. The questions evoke the dialogue and catechism form of certain medieval texts designed for instructive reading, which Thomas may have met in Shakespeare (e.g. *King Lear* I, v, 27 and 34, and III, iv, 152).

p. 15 *The hand that signed the paper*: (*Notebook* version August 1933) Thomas on the whole resisted the fashion in the 1930s for 'political' and 'socially conscious' poetry. This is the only poem in *Collected Poems* that is on an overtly political subject. In its *Notebook* version it was dedicated to Bert Trick, an early Swansea friend and an active member of the left wing of the Labour Party.

p. 16 *Before I knocked*: (*Notebook* version September 1933) The speaker's consciousness predates, not only birth, but conception itself. Several hints in the poem make us think of that speaker as being Christ. But knowing how often Thomas fuses his own and everyman's identity with Christ's, we can equally well take the primary speaker to be the poet, mythologized by analogy with Christ.

p. 18 *My hero bares his nerves*: (*Notebook* version September 1933) The poem is an elaborate conceit. On one level it evokes the physical act of writing: the 'nerves' and 'head' of the poet's sensibility and mind are 'unpacked' in an 'unruly scrawl' onto the 'lovelorn paper', etc. The final line ('He pulls the chain, the cistern moves') and the mechanistic images throughout draw an analogy between this cathartic act of writing and the flushing of an old-fashioned water-closet. A further analogy in the metaphors is with masturbation (another *Notebook* poem of the same year contains the phrase 'cistern sex').

p. 19 *The force that through the green fuse*: (*Notebook* version October 1933) The identification of the world's elemental forces with those which govern the human body, so characteristic of Thomas's poetry, is in itself clear enough. A greater difficulty would seem to lie in the repeated 'And I am dumb to tell . . .' Thomas is possibly emphasizing the irony that, though physically man is one with the universe, he is separated from it by intellectual consciousness. In other words, the lament is not that he is dumb to tell, but that he can conceive of *telling* in the first place. In that sense, 'dumb to tell' also means 'foolish to tell'.

p. 20 *That sanity be kept*: (1933)

p. 21 *In the beginning*: (*Notebook* version April 1934)

p. 22 *Light breaks where no sun shines*: (*Notebook* version November 1933) 'My own obscurity is quite an unfashionable one, based, as it is, on a preconceived symbolism derived, (I'm afraid all this sounds very woolly and pretentious), from the cosmic significance of the human anatomy' (letter to

Glyn Jones, *c.* 14 March 1934). Here Thomas not so much compares as *identifies* the human body with the physical universe – an identification which elementalizes the body and personalizes the universe.

p. 23 *This bread I break*: (*Notebook* version December 1933) The poet's main emphasis is on the irony (pinpointed in the pun on 'break') that the bread and wine which signify and give Christ's *life* in the Holy Communion are made from the *death* of nature. Characteristically, the poem resists man's tendency to abstract significance from an already significant (because vital) world. We remember William Blake's final assertion in *The Marriage of Heaven and Hell:* 'everything that lives is Holy'.

p. 24 *When once the twilight locks*: (*Notebook* version November 1933; thoroughly revised by March 1934) 'I'm enclosing one poem just finished. It's quite my usual stuff, I'm afraid, and quite probably you won't like it. But, honestly, the one "cancer" mentioned *is* necessary.' Thomas's apologetic comment on sending the early version of this poem to Pamela Hansford Johnson in a letter of 11 November 1933 emphasizes how highly characteristic it was of his often morbid concern with the individual's progress from womb to tomb, though mitigated here by the final stanza's healthy commitment to ordinary life. The poem also dramatizes fears and hopes regarding his career as a poet.

p. 26 *Where once the waters of your face*: (*Notebook* version March 1934) 'This new year has brought back to my mind the sense of magic that was lost – irretrievably, I thought – so long ago. I am conscious, if not of the probability of the impossible, at least of its possibility' (letter to Trevor Hughes, early January 1934). The image of a rich and magical sea expresses the wonder and optimism that he feels has faded from his life, just as the image of a dry sea bed suggests the death of his childlike intuitions. As Wordsworth put it in his 'Ode: Intimations of Immortality from Recollections of Early Childhood' – 'Shades of the prison-house begin to close/ Upon the growing boy.'

p. 27 *Our eunuch dreams*: (*Notebook* version March 1934) 'There is no reason at all why I should not write of gunmen, cinemas *and* pylons if what I have to say necessitates it. Those words and images were essential' (letter to Pamela Hansford Johnson, late March 1934). The poem is nevertheless more contemporary in its subject-matter than is usual for Thomas, concerned as it is with the unreal fictions of cinemas as an image for the barren ('eunuch') dreams of adolescence. The theme, however, is highly characteristic. Like the dreams of 'When once the twilight locks' above, the glamorous fictions of cinema deprive us of 'faith' (ll. 29, 36) in the world of actuality.

p. 29 _I see the boys of summer_: (_Notebook_ version April 1934) The poet accuses the 'boys of summer' of suppressing their natural sexuality. These 'boys' can be taken to be the people he sees around him in his immediate community, and in stanzas 3 and 4 they are the unborn children who will become tomorrow's adolescents and adults. Most critics argue that Section II is spoken by the 'boys of summer' themselves, in reply, and that Section III is a line-by-line dialogue between them and Thomas.

p. 31 _If I were tickled by the rub of love_: (_Notebook_ version April 1934) In the first four stanzas the poet imagines four stages of life, respectively those of embryo, baby, adolescent and old man. If he were 'tickled' (either physically or in the sense of being 'amused') by the 'rub' (again, either physical or in Hamlet's sense of 'obstacle') of the experiences associated with those stages of life, he would not fear abstract philosophies, historic events, or death. Instead, 'the only rub that tickles' – that moves him as man and poet – is a morbid fascination with mortality: 'I sit and watch the worm beneath my nail/ Wearing the quick away.' As with Hamlet, this diseased obsession has unfortunately become the very essence of his sensibility. The poem ends with a prayer that full, living humanity become his subject-matter: 'Man be my metaphor.'

p. 33 _Especially when the October wind_: (October 1934) Two major themes come together here. One, stemming from the fact that October was the month of Thomas's birth, is the intimation of decay traditionally associated with autumn. The other, confirmed by similar statements in the letters and by an earlier version of the poem, is what philosophers call the problem of 'nominalism and universals'. That is to say, for Thomas, word and thing seem indivisible: 'When I experience anything, I experience it as a thing and a word at the same time, both equally amazing' (E. W. Tedlock, ed., _Dylan Thomas: The Legend and the Poet_ [Mercury Books, 1963], p. 54).

p. 34 _Should lanterns shine_: (November 1934) The theme is the young man's determination to remain open to experience rather than relentlessly seeking 'answers' or 'solutions' to the mystery of life. As Keats put it in his verse-letter 'To J. H. Reynolds Esq' – 'and to philosophize/ I dare not yet!'

p. 35 *Altarwise by owl-light: Sonnets I, IV and X*: (Sonnet I, finished February 1935; Sonnet IV, September 1935; Sonnet X, finished June 1936) Arguably the most difficult of Thomas's poems, the ten 'Altarwise' sonnets strenuously combine the poet's autobiography with that of Christ, the sexual with the religious, and the flippant or sacrilegious with the proud and momentous. From the 'nativity' of Sonnet I to the 'resurrection' and 'gospel' aftermath of Sonnets IX and X, the sequence includes several aspects of the Christian story – the preaching, fasting and crucifixion – but is highly heterodox in its treatment of them. A major difficulty, beyond understanding the syntax or being able to visualize the images, is that of gauging the tone intended. Refreshingly, Sonnet IV jokes about asking impossible questions ('What is the metre of the dictionary?'), and is a marvellous evocation of the face of an unborn baby in the womb: 'Love's a reflection of the mushroom features.'

p. 37 *O make me a mask*: (*Notebook* version March 1933; rephrased and severely shortened November 1937) The poet seeks to defend his inner privacy against the sharp examination of strangers and critics.

p. 38 *Incarnate devil*: (*Notebook* version May 1933, much revised and shortened for publication in August 1935) A poem about seeing the usual division between good and evil as an idle exercise, superimposed on man's more natural instincts in these things and on the fact that the physical world itself is morally neutral.

p. 39 *How shall my animal*: (March 1938) The 'animal' is a metaphor for inner energies that the act of writing poetry seems both to bring to light and to kill by transferring into words. 'I hold a beast, an angel, and a madman in me, and my enquiry is as to their working, and my problem is their subjugation and victory, downthrow and upheaval, and my effort is their self-expression' (letter to Henry Treece, 16 May 1938).

p. 41 *After the funeral (In memory of Ann Jones)*: (March–April 1938) Ann Jones was the poet's maternal aunt who lived at the farm Fernhill in Carmarthenshire, where Thomas spent so many happy schoolboy holidays throughout the 1920s. After the hypocrisy of the mourners (ll. 1–5) and the emotional poverty of the poet's first response to Ann's death (ll. 7–8), Thomas offers an exaggerated 'Bardic' eulogy which is made to contrast with the old woman's simplicity (ll. 16–20) and with the pious finality of her death (ll. 31–5). A sustained theme is the inadequacy of language to keep human reality alive; but the poem's poignancy lies nevertheless in that attempt.

p. 43 *The tombstone told*: (September 1938) Thomas described this poem as 'Hardy-like' (letter to Vernon Watkins postmarked 14 October 1938), commenting presumably on the oddness of the story on which it is based, that of a girl who died before the sexual fulfilment of her marriage-night. From several time-angles, the poem converges on that event.

p. 44 *On no work of words*: (September 1938) To partake of the created world involves, for the artist, the responsibility of reproducing its creativity in return. From the word 'rich' (l. 2) springs a sustained series of financial imagery: 'gift', 'treasures', 'currencies', 'pay', etc.

p. 45 *Twenty-four years*: (October 1938) Written a few days before the poet's twenty-fourth birthday. The metaphor (ll. 6–9) for setting out on life is that of a young man setting out on a date.

p. 46 *Once it was the colour of saying*: (December 1938) A kind of interim report on the poet's own career. Thomas feels that up to now the glamour of words has meant more to him than the human experience they ought to be exploring.

p. 47 *If my head hurt a hair's foot*: (March 1939) Thomas's first child, Llewelyn, was born in January 1939. Stanzas 1–3 are spoken by an unborn child; Stanzas 4–6 are the mother's reply to the child's fears of causing her pain in birth. 'It is not a narrative, nor an argument, but a series of conflicting images which move through pity and violence to an unreconciled acceptance of suffering: the mother's *and* the child's. This poem has been called obscure. I refuse to believe that it is obscurer than pity, violence, or suffering. But being a poem, not a lifetime, it is more compressed' (from Thomas's comments introducing a reading of his poetry on BBC radio, 24 September 1949).

p. 48 *To Others than You*: (May 1939) The poet's accusation is that friendship has been used as a cover to lay bare his inner privacy. The main syntax runs: 'You . . . Whom now I conjure to stand as thief . . . Were once such a creature . . . [That] I never thought to utter or think . . . That . . . My friends were enemies on stilts . . .'

p. 49 *When I woke*: (July 1939) 'This war, trembling even on the edge of Laugharne, fills me with such horror and terror and lassitude' (letter to Vernon Watkins, postmarked 25 August 1939). Morning village sounds in Laugharne wake Thomas from his private nightmares and to his work as a poet. But a new 'voice in the erected air' of a radio news programme announces a different nightmare – the outbreak of the Second World War.

p. 50 *Paper and sticks*: (autumn 1939) An unusually 'realistic' poem for Thomas at this stage, which is why, having included it in *Deaths and Entrances* in 1946, he later omitted it from his *Collected Poems* in 1952.

p. 51 *There was a saviour*: (February 1940) 'The churches are wrong, because they standardize our gods, because they label our morals, because they laud the death of a vanished Christ, and fear the crying of the new Christ in the wilderness' (letter to Pamela Hansford Johnson, week of 11 November 1933). The poem emphasizes man's *individual* responsibility for love and compassion. In the past, Christianity has been a comforting other-worldly escape from that responsibility. Now, in a less religious age, and in the first winter of the Second World War, human tragedy is brought home to each individual conscience. In this direct confrontation with those who have perverted Christ's teaching, Thomas gains an added irony by using the stanza-form of Milton's Hymn 'On the Morning of Christ's Nativity', which Kathleen Raine recalls was Thomas's favourite poem.

p. 53 *Deaths and Entrances*: (Summer 1940) Thomas called this his 'poem about invasion', and it was written after a particular air raid on London in the summer of 1940 that had a profound effect on him – 'I get nightmares like invasions, all successful' (letter to Vernon Watkins, summer 1940). The 'you' addressed throughout is any person on the 'eve' of actual death in such 'incendiary' raids. A phrase in the third and last stanza – the 'near and strange' casualties of the London raids – helps with the referents of the first two stanzas. 'Near' relates to friends and loved ones, a representative of whom is described in the first stanza as falling into the silence of endless mourning at 'your' death; and 'strange' relates to one who is not actually known to you because he is 'sun [son] of another street' but who is on your side in the war and will sacrifice himself in your defence (an R.A.F. fighter pilot seems intended). But one figure above all will detect and reach you – Death itself, seen in the close-up image of a German airman crashing in the very act of killing you (the letter quoted at the beginning of this note describes a German 'plane brought down in Tottenham Court

Road'). The poem's title is from John Donne's sermon *Death's Duell*: 'Deliverance from that death, the death of the wombe, is an entrance, a delivery over to another death.'

p. 55 *On the Marriage of a Virgin*: (January 1941) The early, longer *Notebook* version (March 1933) had probably been prompted by his sister's forthcoming wedding in May 1933.

p. 56 *Love in the Asylum*: (April 1941) As with the previous poem and 'On a Wedding Anniversary' below, this poem is possibly a spin-off from Thomas's own relatively new marriage. 'Mad' was certainly the word he and his wife Caitlin used jokingly of themselves. But the madness of war's air raids and blackouts is also in the background.

p. 57 *The hunchback in the park*: (July 1941) The hunchback, the warning bell, the chained cup, etc., were for the poet memories of Cwmdonkin Park, close to the poet's birthplace in Swansea. The relationship of the hunchback to the 'figure without fault' (l. 32) which he creates is that between the mortal poet and the created poem: so Thomas here is, all at once, the narrating poet, one of the tormenting boys and the hunchback himself.

p. 59 *Among those Killed in the Dawn Raid was a Man Aged a Hundred*: (July 1941) Characteristically, the sonnet refuses to let the natural triumph of the centenarian's death be obscured by piety, officialese or propaganda. Instead, it records the events with a quiet irony – that such an old man should need to be killed by a bomb. The flat title was an actual headline in a newspaper. With an even crueller irony, Thomas considered, as a title for the second part of 'Ceremony After a Fire Raid' (below) 'Among Those Burned to Death was a Child Aged a Few Hours'.

p. 60 *Lie still, sleep becalmed*: (April 1944) Though the sonnet probably derived from sympathy with the suffering and the dying in wartime, it probably also carried memories of the poet's father suffering from mouth cancer ten years previously.

p. 61 *Ceremony After a Fire Raid*: (May 1944) 'It really is a Ceremony, and the third part of the poem is the music at the end' (letter to Vernon Watkins, 27 July 1944).

p. 64 Poem in October: (August 1944) One of the poet's many birthday poems. The location is Laugharne in Carmarthenshire, viewed (from stanza 3 onwards) from Sir John's Hill. Thomas called it 'a Laugharne poem: the first place poem I've written' (letter to Vernon Watkins, 26 August 1944).

p. 67 Holy Spring: (November 1944) Waking from the marriage bed to a world at war, Thomas rejoices in being alive and singing, 'if only', as the poem says, 'for a last time' (l. 24).

p. 68 The conversation of prayers: (March 1945) The curious music is produced by the mixture of end rhymes with carefully placed internal rhymes (e.g. stanza 1: prayers-stairs-tears, said-bed-dead, love-move, room-whom). Rhymes crossing in this way in the middle of lines is a structural reflection of the main theme – the crossing of two individual prayers.

p. 69 A Refusal to Mourn the Death, by Fire, of a Child in London: (March 1945) Unlike its negative title, the poem's tone is affirmative in this evocation of the child's return into cosmic life. It 'refuses' to fall into pious lament or propaganda.

p. 70 This side of the truth (for Llewelyn): (March 1945) Llewelyn was the poet's son, his first child, aged six when the poem was written. The poem claims that, however man himself may distinguish between Good and Bad, he does so in a completely neutral universe.

p. 72 A Winter's Tale: (March 1945) The phrase 'a winter's tale' traditionally describes a non-realistic story told only in order to while away a winter's night. As in Shakespeare's The Winter's Tale, however, there are tragic dimensions to the story.

p. 77 In my craft or sullen art: (September 1945) A general comment in an essay by W. H. Auden seems a good approximation to the theme of this poem: 'The impulse to create a work of art is felt when, in certain persons, the passive awe provoked by sacred beings or events is tranformed into a desire to express that awe in a rite of worship or homage, and to be fit homage, this rite must be beautiful. This rite has no magical or idolatrous intention; nothing is expected in return' ('Making, Knowing and Judging' in The Dyer's Hand).

p. 78 Fern Hill: (September 1945) Fernhill is a farm a few miles outside Carmarthen in west Wales. Thomas spent many childhood holidays there at a time when it was the home of Ann Jones, the maternal aunt commemorated in 'After the funeral', p. 41. In a letter to David Tennant, 28 August 1945, Thomas said of 'Fern Hill' that 'it's a poem for evenings and tears'. One should note the use of assonance (vowel patternings) instead of rhymes at the line-endings (e.g., Stanza 1: boughs-towns, green-leaves, starry-barley, climb-eyes-light).

p. 80 On a Wedding Anniversary: (September 1945) The different first version (published January 1941) was prompted by the poet's third wedding anniversary.

p. 81 In Country Sleep: (April–July 1947) The poet's daughter (Aeronwy, born March 1943) is enjoined, on going to sleep, not to fear the figures of nursery tales and nightmares. The created world is not a threatening one. The figure to fear – but feared creatively, in an act of recognition – is what the poem calls the 'thief', representing the world of experience and ultimately death. In that sense the poem dramatizes the verse in 2 Peter 3:10: 'But the day of the Lord will come as a thief in the night.'

p. 85 Over Sir John's hill: (May–August 1949) Sir John's Hill is a wooded promontory overlooking the estuary of the rivers Taf and Towy in Laugharne, and the main land feature visible from the shed in which Thomas wrote his late poetry.

p. 87 In the White Giant's Thigh: (November 1949) The poet walks over a 'high chalk hill' (the White Giant of the title) at night, and imagines the former lives of the childless women lying buried there, and the survival of their longings even in death. There is, in fact, a White Giant figure carved in chalk, and associated with fertility superstition, at Cerne Abbas, Dorset, near where Dylan Thomas often stayed with his wife's mother – at Blashford, near Ringwood in Hampshire.

p. 90 Lament: (March 1951) Of all the poems which Thomas included in his *Collected Poems* in 1952, this is the one with the clearest affinities to the comic gusto of the poet's prose works and to the characterization in *Under Milk Wood*. The phrase 'coal black' in each stanza is one of the remaining signs that in an early version in the Humanities Research Centre Library, University of Texas, the poem's title had been 'The Miner's Lament'. Images such as 'the moon shaft slag' and 'the skinbare pit' disappeared from the poem, but 'black spit', 'ram rod', 'wick', etc., still reflect its earlier 'mining' context.

p. 92 *Eli Jenkins's hymn to the morning, from* Under Milk Wood: Thomas was working on the celebrated radio 'Play for Voices' from 1950 to his death in 1953. Eli Jenkins, a gentle poet and Noncomformist minister, is one of the main characters of the play. His morning hymn, like his evening one, is a shrewd but moving parody of amateur verse, its use of Welsh place-names alive with beautiful word-music.

p. 94 *Do not go gentle into that good night*: (March 1951) Addressed to the poet's father as he approached blindness and death. The relevant aspect of the relationship was Thomas's profound respect for his father's uncompromising independence of mind, now tamed by illness. The poet sets himself the task of mastering strong emotion in the difficult form of the villanelle. Five tercets are followed by a quatrain, with the first and last line of the first stanza repeated alternately as the last line of subsequent stanzas and gathered into a couplet at the end of the quatrain – and all this on only two rhymes. The poem has strong echoes of Yeats's favourite words ('rage', 'gay' and 'blaze') and the middle four stanzas, describing the common approach to death of four different types of men, recall the fifth section of Yeats's 'Nineteen Hundred and Nineteen'.

p. 95 *Poem on his Birthday*: (autumn 1949–summer 1951) The poem owes most of its imagery and atmosphere to its location in Laugharne. The 'house on stilts' (l. 4) is either the Boat House where the poet lived or the nearby shed where he did most of his writing at this time. A significant dimension in the poem's imagery ('hammer flame', 'rocketing wind', etc.) is the poet's acute fear of a Third (atomic) World War.

p. 99 *Elegy*: The poet had been working on this elegy to his father (who died 16 December 1952) right up to his departure on his last trip to America in autumn 1953, but it was left unfinished at the poet's own death in America that November. A notebook in the Humanities Research Centre, University of Texas, contains drafts of lines for the poem, along with thirty-three numbered sheets. On sheet 2 is entered the poem as printed here, titled 'Elegy', and representing the stage which the draft materials had so far reached. On sheet 30, Thomas wrote down his original thoughts for the poem:

(1) Although he was too proud to die, he did die, blind, in the most agonizing way but he did not flinch from death & was brave in his pride. (2) In his innocence, & thinking he was God-hating, he never knew that what he was was: an old kind man in his burning pride. (3) Now he will not leave my side, though he is dead. (4) His mother said that as a baby he never cried; nor did he, as an old man; he just cried to his secret wound & his blindness, never aloud.